«Jesus did many other things as well. If every one of them were written down, I suppose that even the whole world would not have room for the books that would be written».
(John 21:25)

«Modern Christianity must be available to welcome the unveiling of the historical figure of Jesus, at any time».
(Albert Schweitzer)

© 2019 Viverealtrimenti Ltd, London
ISBN 978-1-9996689-2-1

www.viverealtrimenti.com

Manuel Olivares

Jesus in India?
One question, several answers

Acknowledgements

This book has been written after a long and challenging period of research, supported by several people and institutions.

First of all I am deeply grateful to the Kashmiri Professor, Maria Fida Hassnain, whose books developed within me, almost twenty years ago, an interest for the "Indian years" of Jesus.

In 2009 I had the chance and privilege to know the Professor personally — who passed away in July 2016 — and develop a fruitful professional relationship.

I would also like to thank friends of the Varanasi *Luminous Bookshop* — Ashish and Shyam — for their advice and their literature once the research has begun.

A special thanks is due to the *Ahmadiyya Muslim Community*, especially to Dr. Aijaz Naik who organized my research stay in Qadian (Punjab; India), Srinagar (Kashmir; India), Patna (Bihar; India) and London where Mr. Arif Khan — editor of the *Tomb of Jesus* website — gave me additional advice.

Mr. Arif Khan has also spent a remarkable amount of time editing this English edition (this book has originally been published in Italian).

A minor contribution to the editing work was provided by my British friend Peter who also deserves to be included in this "list of gratitude".

In Qadian, the holy town of Ahmadiyya where I spent almost three weeks in December 2014, I have been greatly supported by Dr. Nazim Khan and Mr. Zabi Ullah, to whom I express my deepest gratitude.

With the Mission House of *Ahmadiyya Muslim Community*, in Srinagar, where I spent some time before and after my stay in Qadian, I had a fruitful exchange of books and I was able to obtain some rare and precious research material.

While in Srinagar, I was kindly supported by Mr. Zahid Russul. I had the pleasure of spending several hours working with him as well as some casual time, both of which passed pleasantly.

To compile this book I have worked, between 2014 and 2015, in several libraries: *Benares Hindu University* (BHU) library, *The British Library* (incomparable!) in London, Patna's *Khuda Bakhsh Oriental Public Library* and *Biblioteca Nazionale Centrale* in Rome.

As for as the books are concerned, I also received valuable support from my friend Leo, owner of the *Shaman Bookshop* in Chiang Mai (Thailand), where I found some rare material, unavailable in India.

I am even grateful to my dear friend Giulio Di Giuliomaria (who unfortunately passed away on October 2016) who gave me his own personal copy of the rare book *Gesù visse e morì in Kashmir (Jesus lived and died in Kashmir)*, by Andreas Faiber Kaiser.

From a logistical point of view, I'm grateful to Smriti Singh's *Om Yoga Health Society*, in Varanasi, my main base in India, where I had my personal working space and a modest library, enjoying the company of my female four-legged friends: Polio, Chooni and Bianchina and — sometimes — of Nerone (Polio's "partner" and father of Bianchina); street and domestic dogs at the same time.

A great thanks is due to the Dwivedi family (one of its members, Pragya Dwivedi, has authored the book *Ganesh the removal of obstacles* with Viverealtrimenti) who hosted me in their big home in Varanasi.

There I lived with some extraordinary people who would grow to become very dear friends.

I am therefore grateful to Mallik, Neelabh, Maria, Virat, Avinash, Constance, Smriti Agrawal, Rafael, Josiane and to the staff of the house, composed of Ganesh and Rajkumari.

A deep thanks is also deserved or his support during my research by the journalist Alberto Caspani, admin of portal *Altrimenti.net*.

Lastly, an obligatory thanks is due to my parents (for obvious reasons) and to Jalaj Varma, my travel agent in Varanasi, who has showed almost their level of patience, managing my frequent trips and changes of programs during my stay in India.

I hope my efforts will be appreciated by you, kind reader, and that the great figure of Jesus-Issa — whose role in great religious traditions such as Islam, Buddhism and Hinduism is much more important than the average Christian is aware of — could be a constant source of inspiration for the new globally connected human race.

M.O.

CONTENTS

11 Introduction

17 *Druk Amitabha Mountain* 20/10/2014

21 Srinagar…and what's remaining of "milk and honey land" (September 2009)

51 *Druk Amitabha Mountain* 21/10/2014

55 Ladakh (August 2014)

73 Srinagar, five years later (Beginning of September 2014)

77 Varanasi (November-13 December 2014)

83 *The Crucifixion, By An Eye-Witness*

89 Nicholas Notovitch and the disappeared manuscripts

99 Mirzā Ghulām Ahmad and a heterodox Islamic eschatology

123 The esoteric approach; visits of Akashic records

135 Swami Abhedananda's Journey into Kashmir and Tibet

147 N. Roerich and the rich Himalayan oral tradition

151	Qadian 15-29/12/2014
159	Miguel Serrano; from the Andes to the Himalayas on the trail of the Siddha Ashram
167	The Rajneesh Bible and the Pilate's letter to Tiberius
175	Other bibliographical contributions about the Indian years of Jesus
193	Paramahansa Yogananda: the second coming of Jesus
205	The Shroud of Turin – The Burial Cloth of Jesus?
223	Conclusions
229	Appendix
253	Bibliography

Introduction

Jesus in India? I think the question mark is necessary.

The hypothesis that Jesus lived part of his life in India, during the years not mentioned in the Gospels (which present him, as a child, in Jerusalem's temple — where he impressed the rabbis with his wisdom — and then, eighteen years later, at the beginning of his preaching) and after crucifixion, to which, according to some hypothesis, he survived the ordeal, has been argued for a long time.

Multiple versions of the story of Jesus travelling to India exist.

The adherents of this thesis cover a wide range of society, from the common people of India through to the highly educated and political élite.

In Europe the controversial issue of Jesus' Indian years began to be seriously known at the end of the nineteenth century, after the discovery of an ancient manuscript — in the Tibetan language — in a Buddhist monastery of Ladakh (an Indian state bordering with Tibet and known as *small Tibet*).

The discovery was by a Russian journalist and traveller: Nicholas Notovitch.

He was able to have the manuscripts fully translated, discovering details of a long stay by Jesus in the area of modern day India.

Later, he brought the translation to Paris and, then, to Rome.

Vatican authorities, of course, were not enthusiastic about the spreading of Notovitch's discovery — his first book, with partially translated manuscripts, was published in French with title *La vie inconnue de Jésus Christ* (the unknown life of Jesus) — and the author was depicted as a fraud by the most important orientalist of those times: Max Müller.

While in Europe the debate about the unknown life of Jesus was increasing, in Qadian, a small town in the Indian state of the Punjab, another crucial book in the Urdu language was being produced: *Masih Hindustan Mein*.

Translated into English in 1944 with the title *Jesus in India*, it offered a different perspective from the controversial Notovitch's book.

Indeed, *Masih Hindustan Mein* was focusing on a hidden "second life of Jesus", in India (mostly in Kashmir), after he survived the ordeal of Crucifixion.

Less attention, again in relation to the book of Notovitch, was given to a verification travel to the same Ladakhi monastery — approximately thirty years after the visit of the Russian traveller — by one of the most brilliant scholars of contemporary India: Swami Abhedananda.

He was, ironically, a friend of Max Müller.

Swami Abhedananda was the last documented individual to have examined the manuscripts which inspired Notovitch's controversial book.

However, a lot of written material has been produced in the following decades about Notovitch and Mirzā Ghulām Ahmad (author of *Masih Hindustan Mein/Jesus in India*) work.

Other books followed encouraging a lively current of thought — transversal to different religions — finding their homes in relevant niches within Hinduism, Buddhism and Islam.

Even members of the *New Age* movement chose to be involved in the issue of a possible Jesus' stay in India, as well as founders of new religious movements (for instance Osho

Rajneesh, Sathya Sai Baba[1] and Paramahansa Yogananda) and clairvoyants (Edgar Cayce and Levi H. Dowling, to mention only the most famous ones).

In Western countries, today, skepticism predominates but we cannot exclude (with the progression of globalization) the hypothesis that the Indian years of Jesus will be considered more seriously in the future.

The crucial barrier to furthering the area of research is the lack of objective evidence; mostly the manuscripts found by Notovitch are not easily available today.

The alleged tomb of Jesus in Srinagar, Kashmir, is closed to the public. I had an interview with its guardian, Mr. Mohd Amin Ringshawl, who incontrovertibly denied that in the *Rozabal* tomb (name of sanctuary even containing the tomb of Muslim saint Syed Nasir-Ud-Din) is buried the Palestinian Master.

«The fact that Jesus is buried here or wherever in the world», *Rozabal*'s guardian told me, «contradicts what is written in The Qur'an and, therefore, it must be condemned as blasphemy!».

---

[1] «Early in His life He (Jesus) announced, "I am God's Messenger, I have come as a servant to all God's children. Later he retired from the world to be alone and contemplate the nature of God. He was totally immersed in the God within Himself for twelve years. The strength of His singular concentration drew Him much closer to God. By the power of His divine consciousness Jesus grew nearer, nearer and still nearer to God, and realized He was Himself the Son of God. Craving God still more, He went on a pilgrimage to an isolated part of the Himalayan mountains, dwelt even more deeply and constantly in God's Love. He continued this practice for five years. In his mountain retreat He practised a number of intense spiritual disciplines. He realized that the embracing Love of the Father was His own basic nature. He declared, "I and My Father are One". The full awareness of His unity with the Almighty occurred while He was in India».

In: *An eastern view of Jesus Christ, Divine Discourses of Sathya Sai Baba*, Sai Publications, London, 1982, pp. 112-113.

Someone urged a DNA test of the man buried in *Rozabal*.

Despite a good beginning, the operation has not been successful, even because the old town of Srinagar (where the *Rozabal* is located) is one of the hottest points in the world for historical insurrection opposing Kashmiri separatists to the Indian army and the Central Indian Government in New Delhi.

I think the research has to go on regardless of the political situation and the afore mentioned manuscripts could be "rediscovered". If not exactly Notovitch's ones, I think there could be reasonable chances to find similar copies somewhere else. They may have been produced in abundance and, at least, two different languages. As Notovitch writes in his book the manuscripts have been written, originally, in Pali language and, afterwards, they have been translated into Tibetan.

Digging into the apocryphal, Persian, Kashmiri and Hindu literature and considering some archeological data, we will find other paths to follow.

Several pieces of the puzzle have to be found to throw more light on the controversial issue considered in this book, even if some crucial elements could have been hidden fearing a physiological uproar provoked by the discovery of a more complex version of Jesus' life.

I've decided to try to put in order the rich variety of available material, reading several books, carefully surfing the internet, and undertaking my own personal research journey.

I think to proceed on the path of a trans-cultural Jesus — not only the prerogative of the Christian world — could be greatly beneficial for the modern, globalised man.

A trans-cultural Jesus can contribute to reducing the distances between the worlds that still consider themselves, maybe wrongly, very different, and infusing new energy to an undeniably suffering Christian faith.

Finally, I hope this work could be also an interesting travel book, written in part in form of diary.
Enjoy your reading!

Druk Amitabha Mountain 20/10/2014

Sometimes it is necessary to leave. Every non-Indian person living in India — or in any other country requiring a visa for a foreigner to stay — knows that. It is possible, sometimes, to stay longer, to get more generous permits but, inexorably, comes the moment of departure. At the beginning it could be disorienting, then it becomes just a matter of organization.
It is one of the aspects determining the destiny of a nomadic lifestyle.
I've landed in Kathmandu on the fifteenth of October, after almost three months spent in India.
Three very intensive months, on the trail of Jesus' possible stay in the country.
Some people consider this possibility just a legend created by a Muslim heterodox environment.
In general we can say it is discussed with astonishment if not with hostility by most Western people (considering the basis of their belief revolves around the crucifixion and resurrection of Christ as related in the New Testament).
However, as far as I have read and experienced, it is commonly accepted as an integral part of the true story of Jesus by a prominent section of the Indian, educated élite (Pandit Nehru, as we will see, considered it with great interest) and it is also very popular among common people, in India.
For me, everything began in Rome in one bizarre bookshop, around fifteen years ago. At the end of 2005 I had started to live regularly in Varanasi, approximately half way between New Delhi and Kolkata. There I had read Holger

Kersten's bestseller, translated into almost forty languages, *Jesus lived in India* (mentioned in bibliography).

In 2009 I made my first trip to Srinagar, where the supposed "grave of Jesus" can be found. I knew Professor Maria Fida Hassnain, a pioneer of this rich current of studies, and we had an interview.

I wrote the pages you will read in the next paragraph, directly from my travelogue.

Since then, everything had remained in cold storage for some years, even though I had collected more material, mostly from the internet.

Around one year ago, my interest started to grow stronger, when a bookseller, in Varanasi, sold me a copy of *The second coming of Christ*, by Paramahansa Yogananda. I found there, with plenty of details, several passages related to Jesus' possible stay in India.

The desire to delve further into this topic, finally, erupted and I decided to "knock at all possible doors". In August, this year, I visited Ladakh (a region whose role in this big story is crucial), I returned to Srinagar meeting again, after five years, Professor Hassnain, I got one reference letter from him and I joined here, on *Druk Amithaba Mountain*, overlooking Kathmandu, in a Tibetan monastery belonging to the *Drukpa* tradition.

Why here? It will be clarified soon.

It's not easy to find what I am looking for but to follow the traces of great men is always an extraordinary thing to do.

The beauty of this monastery — actually it is more a citadel, composed by several well maintained buildings connected by green boulevards well maintained by professional gardeners — is overwhelming and, I think, it is reminiscent of mythical and mystical Himalayan places such as Shambhala and Shangri-La. This is already enough! It gives a good value to this big journey which does not deserve less than the goal to be achieved: to find the "key" of the great history of Jesus' years in India.

Now, we go back go to the first steps: my first visit to Srinagar which inspired the following pages.

Srinagar…and what's remaining of "milk and honey land" (September 2009)

"No, tell, Taiji, how old, truly? And now a brandy bottle, materialising from nowhere: cheap liquor from the folds of the great warm chugha-coat. Then a shudder, a belch, a glare. Glint of gold. And-at last-speech. "How old? You ask how old, you little wet-head, you nosey…" Tai, forecasting the fisherman on my wall, pointed at the mountains. "So old, nakkoo!". Aadam, the nakkoo, the nosey one, followed his pointing finger. "I have watched the mountains being born; I have seen Emperors die. Listen. Listen, nakkoo…" — the brandy bottle again, followed by brandy-voice, and words more intoxicating than booze — "… I saw that Isa, that Christ, when he came to Kashmir. Smile, smile, it is your history I am keeping in my head. Once it was set down in old lost books. Once I knew where there was a grave with pierced feet carved on the tombstone, which bled once a year. Even my memory is going now; but I know, although I can't read". Illiteracy, dismissed with a flourish; literature crumbled beneath the rage of his sweeping hand. Which sweeps again to chugha-pocket, to brandy bottle, to lips chapped with cold.
Tai always had woman's lips.
"Nakkoo, listen, listen. I have seen plenty. Yara, you should've seen that Isa when he came, beard down to his balls, bald as an egg on his head. He was old and fagged-out but he knew his manners. "You first, Taiji", he'd say, and "Please to sit"; always a respectful tongue, he never called me crackpot, never called me tu either. Always aap. Polite, see? And what an appetite! Such a hunger, I would catch my ears in fright. Saint or devil, I swear he could eat a whole kid in one go. And so what? I told him, eat, fill your hole, a man comes to Kashmir to enjoy life, or to end it, or both. His work was finished. He just came up here to live it up a little".

Mesmerized by this brandied portrait of a bald, gluttonous Christ, Aziz listened, later repeating every word to the consternation of his parents, who dealt in stones and had no time for "gas"»[2].

The driver is having a phone conversation. He travels about sixty km/h and the road is almost empty. Just sometimes we see a couple of headlights behind us, or, more worryingly, in the opposite direction, without any respect for traffic rules.

It is past eleven p.m. It is cold and humid. I turn on the heating in the jeep. I leave the driver to his conversation with his girlfriend even if I should arrive at a decent time in Srinagar.

After few minutes, I ask him to increase the speed.

I am — maybe foolishly — confident I can find, even after midnight, hotels that will be open in town.

We arrive at one checkpoint. On both sides of the road there are two cabins of soldiers, protected by barbed wires and sandbags. Two armed soldiers order us to pull the jeep over.

They require documents. We are four in the jeep. I seat in the front, near the "romantic bearded driver". Behind us is sitting a more bearded guy, dressed in traditional Kashmiri manner and a young Sikh.

We pass through the checkpoint into the remote suburbs of town. In the streets there are only dogs — solitary or in howling packs — and soldiers.

Several, camouflaged long bearded and harsh soldiers. At least in pairs or, some of them also, in small packs. They share with the dogs the night of Srinagar.

I ask the driver to drop me at that *Hotel Paradise*, on the *boulevard*, in front of *Dal Lake*, where it is possible to admire

---

[2]Salman Rushdie, *Midnight's children*, Jonathan Cape, London, 1993, pp. 17-18.

the famous *houseboats*. He agrees but he doesn't know exactly where we are.

Fortunately, the two guests in the jeep intervene, giving the necessary explanations. Then we arrive at the hotel. It is closed. I knock strongly but without result.

«Hotels are closed, at this time, in Srinagar», the driver tells me.

I have learned not to trust the people in India. It is almost impossible they are disinterested. When I was paying my fare, in Jammu, around three hundred kilometers south of Srinagar, the boss of agency pushed me to book a room in one *houseboat*.

«Three hundred rupees only, breakfast included».

However, I did not want to stay in a *houseboat*. After some research I had concluded it was better to stay in a hotel for several reasons. First of all because *houseboats* are very humid and, secondly, they are not very safe in terms of burglary and, last but not least, the guests are not free to move.

In fact, being more or less distant from the shore, to join the city it is necessary to be accompanied, by boat and it is well known *houseboat* owners are particularly greedy, trying to get money, in any way, from their clients. Of course, each generalization is misleading and it is even possible to stay in "five stars *houseboats*", probably advisable for honeymoon couples.

Anyhow, after several attempts I verify that the hotels are truly closed, at this hour, in town.

It is just passed midnight but nobody is answering my insistent knocking.

I am forced to accept the driver's offer to stay in a houseboat, at least for this first night.

We approach a small lake dock, waiting for my host.

He arrives on a small boat; a shadow in the dimly lit night.

He arrives with his assistant who paddles energetically. He arrives smoking grass.

He is humbly dressed, with a salmon colored *kurta pajami* and a simple jacket. He greets me in a friendly manner, passing the joint to the driver who will pass it to an idler on the wharf.

The driver told me the rent to stay in the houseboat was five hundred rupees, even if in Jammu they gave me a lower price.

The most important thing is my host does not try to make the most of the situation, doubling again the rent. Then I forestall him: «In Jammu they proposed for me to stay in houseboat, for three hundred rupees».

«No Sir», he promptly answers, «at least six hundred».

I interrupt him: «they told me three hundred, I will give you five hundred, with breakfast included!».

«Fine, Sir!».

I have been able to bluff, to display self confidence of someone having a good negotiating power while, in reality, he — Raj — was dramatically ahead, because as an alternative to his houseboat I would have had to risk sleeping in the open, in Srinagar's curfew.

India, great school of life, regularly teaches how to behave in these circumstances.

The difference in the price was minimal, but psychologically it is important, in this environment, to protect your own interests and not constantly yield to bargaining pressure.

I jump on the very precarious boat; actually it is a kind of old canoe.

Jarim paddles on the muddy surface of Dal Lake, zigzagging among several houseboats, pseudo-aristocratic and ruined with carved wood verandas and, sometimes, pretentious chandeliers, partially visible from a few open windows.

We arrive at my host's houseboat. Inside it is very welcoming and Kashmiri style, with low, lucid wooden carved armchairs and amaranth colored cushions, a sofa vaguely reminiscent of a triclinium and one beautiful escritoire, again in lucid, carved wood. On the floor lays a huge, sober carpet.

Wooden walls are unadorned, with the exception of a small, silk carpet, hanging as a batik.

Jarim serves some Kashmiri tea in cups on a wooden carved tray. Raj tries to sell me a tour in town, for the next day: five hundred rupees only and he seeks to fascinate me with the idea of a journey to Bandipur, a village where maybe Jesus lived for a while (not far from there it is supposed to be Musa tomb) and where it is possible to visit the cave where he prayed and meditated.

Actually, the suggestive hypothesis of Jesus' stay in Kashmir has been one of the reasons why I am here but I do not like to be bothered and, after drinking tea, I retire to my room.

Its furniture is humbly, in tune with the one of big living room.

On the bed there are no sheets, just dusty, old blankets. I wake up a couple of times, during the night, for the damp cold. Probably, in the bathroom, there is no hot water. Then, even considering Raj's intrusiveness, I have more than one reason to spend just one night on this house-boat.

The day after, in the morning, sitting on veranda, I have "to defend myself" from approaching boatmen urging me to by flowers, refreshments, unnecessarily ornamented and cheap clothes.

I tell Raj I want to leave his place. He tries to show he has no objections but, soon, he starts:

«What's the problem, Sir?!».

I briefly answer: «I need to stay in hotel, please, don't insist!».

«Fine, Sir», but he tries again: «in the morning we will go for a tour in town then we can have lunch here and go to the hotel, without any rush, in the afternoon!».

It is clear he is trying to hold me till late at night to have the chance to say: «Sir, you are tired, sleep here one more night, you can go to the hotel tomorrow!».

Claiming to be the master of my programs, my time, my life, I answer: «Now we go to the hotel, I'll have a shower, shave, settle properly and then we will see what to do!».

«Fine Sir, as you wish, but let me offer another reasonable solution: you can pay just four hundred rupees for the night, I'll give you a better room and I can include, beside the breakfast, even dinner».

I have just placed the baggage in the veranda and, irritated, I answer: «I want to go, please!».

«Fine Sir but it is off season, business is slow, I need money, you cannot help me?».

«No, I am sorry!».

We jump again on the small boat. Jarim paddles again in muddy waters — now in the full light — of Dal Lake.

Other houseboats, Srinagar's "romantic attraction", are often in a poor state, home of underprivileged people.

The general context is almost rotting, despite the indolent and inadequate work of some guys — in a very precarious position on boats crushed by the weight of several dead algae — trying to clean, as they can, the lake's surface.

I find a good hotel on the *boulevard*, beside Dal Lake. In the afternoon I am in a tuktuk: a three wheeled taxi reminiscent of ape-car.

Beside me Fisa, Raj's four years old daughter and Raj himself.

The first stop is on Shankaracharya's hill (traditionally known as Takht-i-Suleiman: the throne of Solomon)[3].

In fact, the famous Indian philosopher and theorist of Vedanta himself is believed to have lived here where he spent his time practicing deep asceticism.

A Hindu temple has been built on the hill; a rarity in this area, which is almost entirely Muslim. The history of this hill and its naming before being called "Shankaracharya's hill" is quite complex, and further information is provided in the Appendix.

Then we visit the famous Moghul gardens, with networks of water channels, reminiscent of Delhi's Red Fort ones, with a beautiful blaze of big, colored flowers and young or elder trees.

We visit a couple of mosques. Raj stops to pray in the first one: Hazratbal Mosque.

I go to the nearby market to taste and appreciate baked goods and some typical street food.

I start eating in the garden, by the lake, of the mosque.

Somebody looks severely at me and I soon discover why: it's the month of Ramadan. I simply did not know it.

Again with Raj and Fisa on the tuk-tuk we arrive at the austere and crowded Jama Majid, the main mosque in town.

There are many beggars — some severely sick, lepers, mutilated — and low quality street food sellers. It is not so pleasant a place. Then we leave again, for the main stop: *Rozabal*.

It is a sanctuary in the old city of Srinagar; perhaps the most dangerous area due to the heavy presence of Kashmiri separatists.

---

[3]«The hill has been known in history by many names — Jeetlark, Gopadri, Takht-i-Sulaiman and Shankaracharya».
You find more information about this interesting issue in the Appendix.

In the modest sanctuary there are the graves of two saints: Syed Nasir-Ud-Din (in the smallest one) and Hazrat Yousa Asaf, Saint Issa, Isha. Different variants of a Hebrew name — Joshua — which did not remain unchanged either in Western lands: Jesu, Jésus, Jesus, Gesù.

Then Jesus could be buried in Srinagar, even if this hypothesis is not at all appreciated by the Catholic Church in Rome and neither by Orthodox Muslims who do not want pilgrims visiting here, bringing a mess in an already very sensitive area. But why should the tomb of Jesus be in Srinagar? It is a long and complex story. I had my first taste of it, as I wrote, in Rome, several years ago, in a bookshop half way between the famous basilicas of Santa Maria Maggiore and San Giovanni. There I have found a book by Maria Fida Hassnain, a Sufi scholar, Kashmiri historian, former director of Jammu and Kashmir Antics Museum and Kashmiri National Archives: *Sulle trace di Gesù l'esseno* (in English: *A Search for the Historical Jesus*). I read it in just two days.

Jesus in India

In his book Professor Maria Fida Hassnain writes he has discovered, after several years of research started in the Indian state of Ladakh, some evidence regarding the "lost years" of Jesus (the ones not mentioned in the Gospels), showing him to have been a great traveller and a universal Prophet.

Hassnain mentions journalist Nicholas Notovitch, born in the Crimea in 1858, who came to India in 1887 and, then, to Ladakh, an area known as small *Tibet* with plenty of Buddhist monasteries (*gompa*).

Through visiting many of the monasteries he collected interesting data regarding the connection, identified by the Lama, between Jesus and Buddhism.

Jesus, known by the Arab name of Issa, was commonly considered Buddha's incarnation and, eventually supported by iconographic and textual evidence, the hypothesis that he lived several years in India became quite reasonable.

Notovitch's most important discovery was the existence of several manuscripts about "Buddha Issa".

They had been several copies, some were Tibetan translations from the Pali original version, preserved in different Buddhist monasteries, in Tibet and Ladakh.

Forced to remain for quite a long period in the Hemis Ladakhi monastery, because he broke one of his legs while he was in the area, Notovitch had been able to see several manuscripts, having them translated by one Lama.

Back in Europe with the translation of the manuscripts, he published them in French, in 1894, with the title *La vie inconnue de Jésus-Christ*, soon translated into English with the title *The Unknown Life of Christ*, in 1895.

Of course his book created some turmoil and, in the Catholic environment, he started to be stigmatized as a fraud.

However, Hassnain writes, before Notovitch a Persian officer of the East India Company, Meer Izzut-Oolah, after his visit, in 1812, to Ladakh, mentioned both Jesus portrayals in Buddhist monasteries and interesting scripture[4].

---

[4] Quoting the most interesting part of Meer Izzut-Oolah's *Travels in Central Asia* (Calcutta, 1872, p. 14):

«When a Lama or great man dies, his body is burned, and a sculptured representation of him placed on his tomb. Some of these figures are said to represent a certain prophet, who is still alive in the waters and forests, the former being under his complete control. From this it would seem

He adds the report that in 1922 Swami Abhedananda — vice-president of the *Ramakrishna Mission*⁵ — visited the Hemis monastery and saw the manuscripts, translating part of them and confirming what Notovitch wrote about more than twenty years before.

From the contents of the manuscripts we know Jesus left Palestine when he was around twelve, carrying out a seven-

---

that they have some conception of the prophet Khizr (on him be peace). Others again consider the figure to represent a prophet who is living in the heavens, which would appear to point to Jesus Christ (on him and on our prophet be peace). The Thibetans consider their scripture to be inspired: this book contains many moral precepts and exhortations to worship God, to fulfill a promise, to speak the truth, to abandon what is evil, and such like. It also commands that "if any man take away thy sheet give him thy cloack also". Again, "if any man strike thee on one cheek tell him to strike the other also". In that book the worship of idols and the ascribing to other than God the attributes of deity is forbidden. With the exception of the custom of burning the dead many of their observances are similar to those of Christians. [...] Their great feast again is held at the time when the sun enters Capricorn, corresponding with the Christmas festival of the Christians. [...]. Another similar custom is, that a man when taking an oath swears by Kunchooghsoom, Kunchoogh meaning God, and sum, three, that is by the three Gods or Trinity. They acknowledge but one God, the other members of the Trinity being a prophet and their sacred book. [...] I was informed by an aged man that he had ascertained beyond all doubt that some portions of the Christian Bible had been revealed to the Thibetans, but that, in consequence of their not being in possession of the whole book, the practice of burning the dead and the doctrine of the transmigration of souls have been admitted as a portion of their practice and faith. The Thibetans assert that their original scripture was in a language now become unintelligible to them, and has been translated into their own tongue. Notwithstanding all my endeavors, I was unable to procure any portion of their sacred book».

⁵Founded, in 1897, by Swami Vivekananda (1863-1902), pupil of Ramakrishna Paramahansa (1836–1886) and famous to have represented Hinduism in World Parliament of Religions, in Chicago, in 1893.

teen years pilgrimage in India, learning from Buddhism and, then, teaching as a master.

We can consider, in detail, Hassnain's reconstruction, realized thanks to the mentioned material and other rare documents.

For instance, the Professor quotes the "Essene version", obtained by the translation and publication — in English in 1873 — of a manuscript belonging to German Freemasonry, which has been, later, boycotted till just one copy survived. Then, a new edition had been published in 1907 with the title *The Crucifixion by An Eye-Witness* (Indo-American Book Co., Chicago, 1907).

The eye-witness was an Essene who, writing to a brother in Alexandria, just seven years after the crucifixion, affirms Jesus grew up in his confraternity who took care of the "holy family" during its escape to Egypt to save the new born child from Herodian persecution.

Considering some characteristics — described by Flavius Josephus — of the Essenes, as the refusal of violence (clashing with the image we can get by Qumran scrolls, especially by the *Rules of war of sons of light against sons of darkness*[6]) — Hassnain considers reasonable the hypothesis that their source of inspiration — in Egyptian territories where missionaries of famous Indian, Buddhist Emperor Aśoka[7] arrived (304 A.C. – 232 A.C.) — was in fact Buddhism.

---

[6]About the Essenes the great historian of religions Mircea Eliade writes: "the members of community refrained from marriage because they were considering themselves as soldiers ready to fight a holy war".

[7]Ashoka, also spelled Aśoka, (died 238? BCE, India), last major emperor in the Mauryan dynasty of India. His vigorous patronage of Buddhism during his reign (c. 265–238 BCE; also given as c. 273 232 BCE) furthered the expansion of that religion throughout India.

[...]

Hassnain is not the only supporter of this hypothesis. Several scholars consider it (more or less) reasonable even if, very often, Essenism is identified with a Palestinian school while in Egypt it is accepted, in the same historical period, the existence of the Therapeuts, who are similar to Essenes[8] but with their own, autonomous identity.

Egypt, in Jesus' period, was characterized by much religious syncretism. Old Alexandria, in fact, with its very rich and famous library was a center of confluence of the most important, contemporary currents of thought.

He took strong measures to suppress schisms within the sangha (the Buddhist religious community) and prescribed a course of scriptural studies for adherents.
The Sinhalese chronicle Mahavamsa says that when the order decided to send preaching missions abroad, Ashoka helped them enthusiastically and sent his own son and daughter as missionaries to Sri Lanka. It is as a result of Ashoka's patronage that Buddhism, which until then was a small sect confined to particular localities, spread throughout India and subsequently beyond the frontiers of the country.
(*www.britannica.com/biography/Ashoka*)
[8]Jewish historian Flavius Josephus has written extensively, in *Antiquities of the Jews* and in *Jewish war* about them.
Quoting one passage of *Antiquities of the Jews*:
«The doctrine of the Essenes is this: That all things are best ascribed to God. They teach the immortality of souls, and esteem that the rewards of righteousness are to be earnestly striven for; and when they send what they have dedicated to God into the temple, they do not offer sacrifices because they have more pure lustrations of their own; on which account they are excluded from the common court of the temple, but offer their sacrifices themselves [...].
[...] [They have] all things in common; so that a rich man enjoys no more of his own wealth than he who hath nothing at all. There are about four thousand men that live in this way, and neither marry wives, nor are desirous to keep servants; as thinking the latter tempts men to be unjust, and the former gives the handle to domestic quarrels; but as they live by themselves, they minister one to another».(AJ 18.1.5)

Going back to the historical reconstruction of the Kashmiri author, either Notovitch's book, either one *sutra* called *Natha Namavali* affirms Jesus, in his thirteenth year, left for India.

Moreover, roads connecting the Middle-East to India — coinciding, in part, with the ones German geographer Ferdinand von Richthofen identified, in 1877, with the famous *Silk Road* — were already covered with the expansion of the empire of Alexander in the fourth century B.C.

A more detailed perspective on this topic is given by economist, philosopher, Harvard Professor and Nobel Prize for Economy in 1998 Amartya Sen:

«One of the dominant influences in understanding the contact and intercourse between Asia and Europe is the impact and influence of what is called the Silk Route. Extending over 4000 miles, this was the route through which merchandise moved between Asia and Europe. Silk was one of the principal exports of China — hence the name. Originally established between the third century BC and the third century AD, during the Han Dynasty, the Silk Route was of profound importance not only for trade and commerce, but also for intermingling of people and ideas. [...]

If trade gets people together (and it certainly does), then so does interest in knowledge and enlightenment. Mathematics, science, engineering and the arts, along with religious and ethical commitments, have moved the people across regions, by land and across the seas, in pursuit of human interest in them.

The important point is that the motivation behind these journeys was not the pursuit of commercial gains, but search for ideas.

The huge popularity of seeing global connections only through the prism of trade, of which the Silk Route is a leading example, should not be allowed to eclipse the fact that reflective engagements have also moved people across countries and regions over millennia»[9].

---

[9]In: Amartya Sen, *The country of the first boys*, Oxford University Press, New Delhi, 2015, pp. 254-255.

Considering again the reconstruction done by Hassnain, in India Jesus was in touch with the Jainas, was initiated into Vedic literature and then lived with Buddhist monks, in Nepal. After a few years he was considered, in the Nepali Buddhist world, a *Bodhisattva*.

Going back to Palestine, he stopped for a while in Persia.

In a second time, writes Hassnain, Jesus probably visited Great Britain, as it is written in a letter by S. Augustine of Canterbury to Pope Gregory the Great.

From the letter emerges Jesus had founded a temple in Glastonbury, a place related with the tradition of the Holy Graal[10].

Hassnain writes Jesus visited Great Britain (probably around 26-27 A.C.) to investigate some secrets of Druidism, particularly flourishing at that time.

After a short introduction to the "lost years of Jesus", we can consider the mystery of death and Resurrection.

Hassnain mentions the *quérelle* about the Holy Shroud, an object of several scientific investigations.

---

[10] Rev. C. C. Dobson — M.A. Vicar of St. Mary in the Castle, Hastings — in his book *Did our Lord Visit Britain as they say in Cornwall and Somerset* reports the contents of the letter:

«In the Western confines of Britain there is a certain royal Island of large extent, surrounded by water, abounding in all the beauties of nature and necessaries of life. In it the first Neophites of Catholic Law, God beforehand acquainting them, found a Church constructed by no human art, but by the hands of Christ Himself, for the salvation of His people. The Almighty has made it manifest by many miracles and mysterious visitations that He continue sto watch over it as sacred to Himself, and to Mary, the Mother of God».

Rev. C.C. Dobson, *Did our Lord Visit Britain as they say in Cornwall and Somerset,* The Avalon Press, Glastonbury, 1947, p. 24.

He writes that from the analysis of bloodstains on the Shroud, there appeared the existence of serum borders, then of active fibrin in a flowing liquid, impossible to be found in the body *post-mortem*.

Of course Hassnain supports the hypothesis produced by this kind of considerations, opening new scenarios related to Jesus' history.

There does in fact exist a large amount of literature covering the post-Crucifixion years of Jesus.

These texts have in common a view that the crucifixion of Jesus was incomplete and he did not die as a result of this ordeal. This view is supported in the Essene document mentioned previously, believed to be one of the earliest original sources.

Reading this document, Jesus, removed from the cross with vital functions almost imperceptible but still active, was relayed — as it is confirmed in the *Gospel of John* — to Joseph of Arimathea and Nicodemus, both members — and here we're already in front of a heterodox interpretation — of the confraternity of the 'Eye-Witnesses'.

Joseph and Nicodemus, having crucial medical knowledge, used one extraordinary ointment (prepared with myrrh and aloe, mentioned in *Avicenna Canon* and in many other medical Islamic books as *Marham-i-Isa*: the ointment of Jesus)[11] to put

---

[11] We find a mention of herbs healing, mythically, Jesus even in the West, as we can read in following passage of Mircea Eliade's book: *Cosmos and history, the myth of eternal return*:

«As for the magical and pharmaceutical value of certain herbs, it too is due to a celestial prototype of the plant, or to the fact that it was first gathered by a god. No plant is precious in itself, but only through its participation in an archetype, or through the repetition of certain gestures and words which, by isolating it from profane space, consecrate it. Thus two formulas of incantation, used in England in the sixteenth century at the gathering of simples, state the origin of their therapeutic

on the body in the sepulcher. After three days (or, maybe, some more, they could be just three *symbolic* days) they found him in better conditions and took him toa house of the Order.

Hassnain quotes the *Gospel of John* — where it is written Joseph and Nicodemus where at Golgota carrying with them fine linen, myrrh and aloe — and the *Gospel of Luke* — where it is also mentioned the presence of ingredients for an ointment in their bags — as possible confirmation of the Essene version.

It is possible to find hypothesis of Jesus' survival the crucifixion even among Muslims (and among Gnostics and Manicheans).

The historian Abu Huraira[12], in a collection of sayings and teaching of Holy Prophet, published in 1836 with title *Kanz-*

---

virtue: they grew for the first time (i.e., ab origine) on the sacred hill of Calvary, at the "center" of the Earth:
Haile be thou, holiehearbe, growing on the ground;/all in the mount Caluarie first wert thou found./Thou art good for manie a sore, and healestmanie a wound;/in the name of sweet Jesus, I take thee from the ground.
Hallowed be thou, Vervein [verbena], as thou growest on the ground,/for in the Mount of Calvary, there thou wast first found./Thou healedst our Saviour Jesus Christ, and staunchest his bleeding wound;/in the name of [Father, Son, Holy Ghost], I take thee from the ground.
The effectiveness of these herbs is attributed to the fact that their prototypes were discovered at a decisive cosmic moment (*in illo tempore*) on Mount Calvary. They received their consecration for having healed the Redeemer's wounds. The virtue of gathered herbs is effective only insofar as the person gathering them repeats this primordial gesture of cure. This is why an old formula of incantation says: "We go to gather herbs to put them on the wounds of the Lord"».

(Mircea Eliade, *Cosmos and history, the myth of eternal return*, Harper & Brothers, New York, 1959, pp. 30-31)

[12]I quote by the second number of publications of Centre of Islamic Culture in Paris:

ul-Aimal, writes that after he has been saved, Jesus lived a particular odyssey under the guidance and the protection of Allah.

In The Qur'an — *sura* 4, verses 157-158 — it is written:

«They say: "We have killed the Messiah, Jesus, the son of Maryam, the Rasool[13] of Allah". Whereas in fact, neither did they kill him nor did they crucify him but they thought they did *because the matter was made dubious for them*. Those who differ therein are in doubt. They have no real knowledge, they follow nothing but merely a conjecture, certainly, they did not kill him (*Jesus*). Nay! The fact is that Allah took him up to Himself. Allah is Mighty Wise».

There are several Muslim legends identifying a kind of double crucified instead of Messiah who was raised, it is written in The Qur'an, with all his body, in Heaven.

«Abu Hurairah belonged to the tribe of Daus, in Yemen. He came as late as the year 7H./628 to Medinah and embraced Islam; nevertheless he knew more Hadith than many of those who embraced Islam earlier. [...]
Abu Hurairah not only knew reading and writing — then a rare quality — but had also great literary aptitude. He had learned Persian and apparently also Abyssinian, he is said to have known well the contents of the Bible.
The Holy Prophet was also very much impressed by the intellectual advance of Yemen over the rest of Arabia, for when a Yemenite delegation came to Medinah to embrace the Faith, he exclaimed: "The faith (imán) is Yemenite, the law (fiqh) is Yemenite, the wisdom (hikmat) is Yemenite". This is not surprising when one remembers the fact the culture and civilization in Sabá (Sheba) and Ma'ín (Yemen) had reached the pinnacle of its fame hundreds of years before the founding of Rome or even Athens».
(In: *Publications of Centre Cultural Islamique*, Paris, n. 2, 1961, pp. 36-37).

---

[13] Messenger of Allah.

Then Muslims refuse to believe one prophet of God could have suffered the infamy of crucifixion which, even for the Jewish, was a very cruel death, deserved only by real criminals.

Still amongst the Islamic sources, there is a book, published in 1908, whose title could not be more explicit: *Jesus in India (Masih Hindustan Mein)* by Mirza Ghulām Ahmad, founder of the famous *Ahmadiyya Muslim Community*.

It will be considered, in depth, in a separate chapter.

Mirza Ghulām Ahmad writes Jesus, after he survived the crucifixion, followed the traces of the Lost Tribes of Israel, up to Kashmir.

As a proof of this long journey, Mirza Ghulām Ahmad mentions the existence, in Srinagar, of the tomb of prophet Yuzu Asaph who he proposed was Jesus himself.

Mirza Ghulām Ahmad even considered affinities between the figures of Jesus and Buddha and respective spiritual paths. Both, he emphasizes, are tempted by the "devil" and teach through parables, some of them amazingly similar in Christian and Buddhist traditions.

One example is the parable of the lavish son, proposed, even in a slightly different manner, in the *Gospel of Luc* and in *Lotus' Sutra*.

Mirza Ghulām Ahmad highlights both Christian and Buddhist monastic traditions are rooted in three vows of poverty, chastity and obedience.

Returning to the research of Hassnain, he paid more than one visit to the tomb of Yuzu Asaph.

Inside the sanctuary he found one wooden cross and, mostly, one stone slab which, cleaned by the mud, revealed, in bas-relief, two footprints.

He then commissioned an employee of the State Museum to make a plaster mould of the slab. The amazing discovery after deeply examining both the objects, were the marks of two small pads under the feet (possibly used to avoid the inflammation of their scars, during long hours of walking).

Not to be superficial, Hassnain contacted Kurt Berna, a German doctor and scholar who spent a long time studying the Shroud and was a supporter — with scientific proof — of the hypothesis that "Jesus was buried whilst still alive".

He produced a report that highlighted, by the analysis of a reproduction of the wounds, that it was possible to deduct that the man had the left foot based on the right one at the moment of crucifixion. Berna writes in his report:

«[…] The examination of the foot-prints, reveals that these are not the real foot-prints of the man but the stone carver, knew the facts of crucifixion. As such, he wanted to give prominence to the fact of piercing of feet, through nail, by distinguished marks. He knew that the man had been put on the cross and his feet had been pierced, which bore nail marks. Accordingly, he carved the soles of the feet with these distinguished signs.

[…] It is a fact that when these feet impressions are compared with the Holy Shroud of Jesus Christ at Turin, we find that there also the crucifixion was done with left foot put over the right foot and then the nail was struck. After minute examination of the Shroud, it transpires that the left knew was more stiff and bowed like the right leg.
Finally, the indication is that the man in the Holy Shroud at Turin and the man buried in the Tomb at Srinagar, are just the same»[14].

Finally, about Jesus' stay in Kashmir, Hassnain quotes a Sanskrit manuscript, *Bhavishya Maha Purana*, deeply studied in Poona *Oriental Research Institute* and published, in Mumbai, in 1910 (the original version dates from 115 C.E.).

---

[14]Maria Fida Hassnain, *The Fifth Gospel*, Dastgir Publications, Srinagar (Kashmir-India), 1988, pp. 228-229.

It includes the report of a meeting, in Kashmir — probably occurred before 78 C.E. — between the king of a people known as Saka and a holy man claiming to be the "Son of God born of a virgin".

The words of the holy man to the king will reveal a monotheistic message with a clear pagan echo:

«The king asked, "Who are you sir?".
"You should know that I am Isha Putra, the Son of God", he replied blissfully, "and 'am born of a virgin.'"
"I am the expounder of the religion of the mlecchas and I strictly adhere to the Absolute Truth". Hearing this the king enquired, "What are the religious principles according to your opinion?".
Hearing this questions of Shalivahana, Ishaputra said, "O king, when the destruction of the truth occurred, I, Masiha the prophet, came to this country of degraded people where there are no rules and regulations. Finding that fearful irreligious condition of the barbarians spreading from Mleccha-Desha, I have taken to prophethood".
"Please hear, Oh king, which religious principles I have established among the mlecchas. The living entity is subject to good and bad contaminations. The mind should be purified by taking recourse of proper conduct and performance of japa [meditation on the chanting of the holy names of God]. By chanting the holy names one attains the highest purity. Just as the immovable sun attracts, from all directions, the elements of all living beings, the Lord of the Surya Mandala [solar planet], who is fixed and all-attractive, and attracts the hearts of all living creatures. Thus by following rules, speaking truthful words, by mental harmony and by meditation, Oh descendant of Manu, one should worship that immovable Lord".
"Having placed the eternally pure and auspicious form of the Supreme Lord in my heart, O protector of the earth planet, I preached these principles through the mlecchas' own faith and thus my name became 'isha-masiha'".

After having read the book of Maria Fida Hassnain, many other interesting events happened, leading me, again and again, on the path of possible Jesus' stay in India.

Since 2005 I have started to spend, for around thirteen years, most of my time in Varanasi, in the North-West of India and another book, as I wrote, has aroused a great interest in me: *Jesus lived in India*, by the historian of religions Holger Kersten, on the path opened by Professor Hassnain.

Kersten got permission, from the Kashmiri authorities, in 1984, to open the *Rozabal* sarcophagus.

However, the day before the one agreed for the opening, there were some riots in the area of the sanctuary and seven people died. The opening of sarcophagus, then, has been postponed in time but, at the end, nothing happened anymore. Kersten, at the end of his book, does not advise anybody to venture into the old town of Srinagar, searching for the *Rozabal*. Me also, at the beginning, I had some doubts but I was more than determined to visit the sanctuary.

Again in Srinagar and short visits in the land of milk and honey

Raj, of course, does not miss the chance to appear as indispensable. While we are on the way to the *Rozabal* he tells me last time he was there, with a small group of tourists, some soldiers told them rudely to vacate the area. He even tells me the sanctuary has been closed for a few years. This, of course, disappoints me.

Raj even confirms the old town is the most dangerous area in Srinagar and it is not advisable to pay a visit there alone.

I left with the spirit of somebody making a pilgrimage, knowing "some risks are included in the package".

We arrive at the *Rozabal*. The taking of any photos is forbidden.

One board, on the door, quotes verses 157-158 of fourth Qur'anic Surah (I've already reported them in the former paragraph). It also mentions one passage of Matthew's Gospel, on the same board.

Everything contributes to create a kind of mysterious atmosphere.

It is not clearly written that the sanctuary contains Jesus' body.

Two saints are mentioned as buried inside: Syed Nasir-Ud-Din and Hazrat Yousa Asif al Hisa, without identifying the last one as the founder of Christianity.

Even the name does not help to clarify because Jesus, in Arabic, is called Issa, in Persian Yuz/Yuzu while Hindus call him Isha.

The two Qur'anic Surahs, mentioned on the board, do not look to have any direct link with the body that is, according to legend, contained in the sanctuary but according to the Ahmadiyya perspective, as it has been explained to me by Mr Arif Ahmed Khan, Deputy Editor – Christian Section of *The Review of Religions* Magazine of *Ahmadiyya Muslim Community*, those verses prove that Jesus was not Crucified and that he was instead lifted up to heaven.

This all comes down to interpretation and an equally valid interpretation (Ahmadi belief, and supported by some non-ahmadis as well) is that a) he survived the crucifixion and that b) his status was 'raised' (Arabic word *Ra'faa*) by him being saved from the curse of dying on the cross.

From one small window it is possible to see both tombs and it is supposedly the bigger of the two is believed to be the one of "Jesus".

I am there again the day after. I arrive on foot from the Malik hotel, on the *Boulevard*, where I am staying in a room.

I cross, longitudinally, a big section of old Srinagar. I stop in a *bakery*, tasting a couple of special, fresh and crumbly puffs.

I do not feel a particular tension in the air, even if there is a big presence of soldiers and barbed wire.

Again in the *Rozabal*, I can enter in a small room from where I could gain access to the sanctuary if the door was not, unfortunately, locked. I sit going into deep meditation.

The *Rozabal* does not seem to attract a lot of people but I share the small room with one man and one woman.

They are both very simple.

The woman does not remain a long time. She kneels in front of a locked door. She prostrates several times, kissing the threshold of the room. She weeps in devotions.

Even the old man, sitting beside me, prostrates kissing the base of a small window from which it is possible to see the two tombs.

He also sheds tears of devotion. Then he looks at me with languid and doe-like eyes, offering a date. I ask him who's buried in the sanctuary. He does not speak English but opens his hands, miming Jesus on the cross. He points to his feet and, then, in the direction of the biggest tomb where the foot prints of Jesus can be found.

I leave the place and curiosity is "eating me up".

Before I left for Srinagar I found, online, the e-mail address and telephone number of Maria Fida Hassnain.

I phone him without big expectations but he answers quickly:

«Hello, Professor Maria Fida Hassnain?».

«Yes, it's me, who's speaking?».

I introduce myself, I tell him I have read his book, translated into Italian and I am interested in Jesus' stay in India and that, at the moment, I am near the *Rozabal*. He invites me to his home. He asks me to take a *tuk-tuk* and to make him speak with the driver to explain the way. It is unnecessary to state that his invitation fills me with joy. After around one hour I am in the Professor's home, in a suburb of Srinagar. It is a simple but welcoming one. I have Kersten's book with me. He takes me to his study. He has the material of his researches on a low table; several posters where he has pasted magazine clippings, photocopies of letters, the passage, in Sanskrit, of the *Bhavishya Maha Purana* relevant to Jesus' stay in India, etc. He tells me the research is on stand-by, that Holger Kersten has disappeared and that he himself is now old (he is eighty-three) and that new scholars should go on, having all his support.

«Religions are blind», he says, «people must believe, followers, believers, devotees must just believe, they cannot have any question!».

«At the same time», he continues, «we are all waiting for somebody, one new Messiah, one Buddha Maitreya, somebody able to free us from our troubles. However, nobody is ready to acknowledge the truth about *Rozabal*, neither Christian institutions, nor Muslim ones, the sanctuary is, now, closed and nobody wants anyone to go there».

He gives me a copy of his, self-printed, book: *The Rozabal, beyond the da Vinci code*.

He brings me into a small terrace, immediately accessible from the study.

On the floor there are plaster casts reproducing Jesus' foot prints.

I could not take photos of the original ones, inside the sanctuary, so I took a lot of photos on the Professor's terrace.

I soon leave Hassnain's home, going to the *Mughal Darbar*, a good restaurant in Srinagar, to eat a traditionally Kashmiri dish: *Rogan Josh*, curry spiced lamb.

On the road I am amazed by a large presence of female beggars. Several of them are integrally covered by a *bourka*.

I am impressed by other characteristics of the town, anomalous to be an Indian one.

It feel like a more structured area; in several Indian towns, for instance, there is the chronic problem of money changing.

Few, among *rickshaw* or *tuk-tuk* drivers, shop keepers, coolies in the stations have change.

This issue becomes a real problem when typically each time it is necessary to pay twenty or thirty Indian Rupees yet you have only a one hundred rupee note.

In this situation it is necessary to find a way to exchange your note for some smaller currency.

I remember facing this problem even in the Delhi tube while paying for a ticket.

In Srinagar I have rarely suffered for this reason.

I have found a more honest attitude and more cleanliness and I felt it was a more integrated community, even if more noticeably masculine.

The women are, in fact, the subjects paying most for this integration.

It is well known a man, in Muslim society, can have several wives, if he is able to guarantee the same rights for all.

Other men's wives cannot be desired because they are veiled.

Eroticism is, then, almost banned by the roads of this town, with the exception of some vibrant glances, furtive under the veils. This balances another factor of disorder in India: severe sexual repressions coupled with the mostly unanimously recognized as a strong attractiveness of Indian women; beautiful, intense, welcoming and sweet but, not rarely, almost indomitable. With long, well maintained black hair, soft faces, sometimes irresistible glances, having almost the power to "swallow" those who look at them.

Indeed India is ancestrally female but the strong sexuality cannot be expressed freely, especially with long-standing institutions difficult to overcome, such as arranged marriages.

Muslims, through polygamy and the negation — for women — of a public unveiled life, have maybe been able to better contain the consequences of some hormonal hails.

Ninth of September — my birthday — and I need to leave Srinagar. I board a government bus, joining the mountains of nearby Gulmarg, amazed by the proverbial beauty of this Himalayan paradise.

Mountains are green with plenty of forests and crystal-clear water.

During a second visit out of town, to Pahalgam, "the village of the shepherd" — where Jesus, according to Hassnain, may have lived for a while — I discover why Kashmir was considered, again by the Kashmiri Professor, as the real promised land "flowing with milk and honey"(Exodus, 3:8).

In fact, observing the rushing flow of Pahalgam's river, I notice the milky color of the water.

It could really look like a river of milk, probably because of the chromatic effect of stones, on the bottom, with geological and mineralogical peculiarities giving to water a singular color.

Pahalgam nourish me with silence and sweet memories, stimulating in me the desire to return to this corner of India, finding a *sui generis* Jesus, traveller, meditator, master.

A charismatic man who came here, from Palestine, collecting anecdotes and information in the "Esperanto of caravanserais", in front of campfires, sitting with merchants of different provenances with whom he was sharing his journey.

In this moment I think it is not so important to explain, scientifically, who Jesus really was. Too much time has passed, too many interests and instances, even legitimate, of social control stratified on his figure. No more of a man but a symbol. Symbolic of a great culture, a kaleidoscopic civilization that with important historical merits but also responsibility for heinous crimes, has crossed time…till today.

Then, maybe, I think it is good that the sanctuary of *Rozabal* remains closed, left to the pure innocence of the local devotees.

I am happy, at the moment, just with a literary version of the great Palestinian master's life, to feel him closer to my sensibility, to my research.

Convinced, however, that when the time will be ready for revelations, we will get them, as in the cases of Qumran and Nag Hammadi.

And Raj? I have been a guest, for dinner, on his houseboat, coming back from Gulmarg. I ate in a mediocre manner and I saw, crossing precarious scaffold, where he really lives with the family; with his daughter Fisa, the beautiful and discreet wife and two more children.

They live in a small cabin beside the houseboat. It is a four-five square meters kitchen. Raj's wife is often cooking for the guests on the houseboat.

On the floor lay three mats, the blankets lovingly tucked in around Raj's three children.

«We live here», he tells me and I see there is no space for the fridge which is in the living-room.

«I am panicking», he tells me when we are back in the main local of the houseboat.

«I have no money, nothing to buy clothes for my children!».

He smokes in a compulsive manner.

Jarim's face has pictured upon it the same desperation.

I'd like to leave some money, of course. He tries to sell me a silky carpet, hanging (on the wall) as a batik.

It clearly shows signs of age as well as wear and tear.

I tell him I was just thinking of buying a carpet, exactly of that size and I can buy that one, to take home something with a history, stimulating memories (even if melancholic) and which has been a vehicle of "Christian" help!

We agree on four thousand rupees. Raj tells me he had paid the equivalent amount of five thousand rupees, in Turkey, nine years before for the carpet. So I did not get a good bargain in the end but it is ok.

I try to take it but he stops me: «No Sir, leave it here, it is yours but I will bring it, tomorrow, in your hotel».

The day after I wait, in vain, for the carpet. I phone Raj, he gives me more than one appointment without respecting any. I decide to buy a carpet somewhere else. I receive a phone call from his wife, just before I am going to a carpet shop. She needs the telephone sim card she lent to me so that I could use the mobile (in Kashmir common Indian telephone sim cards don't work). I ask, of course, about Raj and the carpet.

«It is very expensive that carpet», she answers.

Then Raj has changed his mind, without telling me, and just missing more than one appointment.

What about his panic? Probably he has found some money somewhere else.

Raj; I see him again in my memories, in his troubled manner, the continuous, nervous movement of his legs, his cigarettes smoked in a compulsive way.

The smell of cannabis pervaded when we were introduced to each other. His mostly aristocratic houseboat and the deep poverty he is living in with his family. His tiresomeness, his incoherence, yet I felt we had something in common, I was almost feeling in him a distant shadow of the great Palestinian master who he had immediately told me about, on his small boat, on the night of my arrival in Srinagar.

I leave Srinagar with the feeling of having glimpsed what the great Russian painter and traveler Nicholas Roerich called the "Heart of Asia".

A territory upon the crossroads of many influences: Hindustani, Buddhist, Chinese, Persian...all under the unmistakable sign of the crescent, in the echo of the *adhān* (Islamic call to worship).

An Orient fabled and elusive, treacherous and tragic.

The Orient, indeed, I have always looked for and I found, almost in a dream, in the dangerous and well-integrated old city of Srinagar. In fragrant pastries, on a gloomy day, of a loyal baker, who did not treat me as a stranger — trying to apply surcharges or looking at me with resentment, distrust, rejection — and that, when I had to pay eight rupees and I took out a banknote of five hundred rupees, did not have the usual disarming expression: no change?

Druk Amitabha Mountain 21/10/2014

We go back to Nepal, on our beautiful mountain, with one specific sentence from Anand Coomaraswamy's book *Buddha and the Gospel of Buddhism* etched in my mind:

«Great things are done when men and mountains meet
They are not done by jostling in the street»[16].

Why on this mountain? Why Amitabha?
I start answering the second question, introducing Amitabha while quoting some sentences from Coomaraswamy's book:

«The Sambhogakaya is the Buddha or Buddhas regarded as God in heaven, determined by name and form, but omniscient, omnipresent, and within the law of causality, omnipotent. A Buddha, in this sense, is identical with the Brahmanical "Isvara", who may be worshipped under various names (e.g. as Vishnu or as Siva), the worshipper attaining the heaven ruled by him whom he worships, though he knows that all of these forms are essentially one and the same. The Mahayana[17] does in fact multiply the number of Buddhas indefinitely and quite logically, since it is the goal of every individual to become a Buddha.
[...]
Amitabha Buddha rules over the heaven Sukhavati, the Pure Land or Western Paradise.

---

[16]Ananda K. Coomaraswamy, *Buddha and the Gospel of Buddhism*, G.P. Putnam's Sons, New York, 1916, p. 170.
[17]Quoting by *Oxforddictionaries.com*: One of the two major traditions of Buddhism, now practised especially in China, Tibet, Japan, and Korea. The tradition emerged around the 1st century AD and is typically concerned with personal spiritual practice and the ideal of the Bodhisattva.

With him are associated the historical Gautama as earthly emanation, and the Bodhisattva Avalokitesvara as the Saviour.

The history of Amitabha relates that many long ages ago he was a great king, who left his throne to become a wanderer, and he attained to Bodhisattvahood under the guidance of the Buddha, that is, the human Buddha then manifest; and he made a series of great vows, both to become a Buddha for the sake of saving all living things, and to create a heaven where the souls of the blessed might enjoy an age-long state of happiness, wisdom and purity.»[18].

Tibet, twelfth century A.D.: Bodhisattva Avalokitesvara manifests himself as a pupil of *Mahasiddha*[19] Lingchen Repa (1128-1188), within the lineage of big saints Tilopa, Naropa, Marpa and Milarepa.

He manifests himself as Protector of beings in the person of Drogon Tsangpa Gyare (1161-1211).

In 1206 he's in Nam-gyi-Phu, not far from Lhasa, searching an auspicious place to build a monastery.

Nine dragons, identified as manifestation of Indian *Mahasiddha*, rise from the earth to sky, with the strong sound of thunder. Considering it a favourable sign, Drogon Tsangpa Gyare names his lineage and his future followers *Drukpa*: Dragons.

The monastery, built *in loco*, realising the prophecy of Lingchen Repa, is named *Namdruk* (Dragons of sky).

To following incarnations of Drogon Tsangpa Gyare is given the title of *Gyalwang Drukpa* and the acknowledgement of lineage's leader.

Drukpa school is soon successful. It takes root in different Tibetan territories, after the planned dispersion of several pupils, dividing in: *To Druk*, "High *Drukpa*", in the West; *Me*

---

[18]Ananda K. Coomaraswamy, *Buddha and the Gospel of Buddhism*, op. cit., pp. 246-247.
[19]Ascetics, in *Vajrayana Buddhism*, having complete control of Tantric teachings.

Druk, "Low *Drukpa*", in the East and *Bar Druk*, "Central *Drukpa*", in the middle.

Since 1300, *Drukpa* starts to take root in Bhutan. In 1651, Shabdrung Ngawang Namgyal, considered the reincarnation of fourth *Gyalwang Drukpa* Kunkhyen Pema Karpo, unifies Bhutan, becoming its spiritual and political guide. He names the country *Druk* and population *Drukpa*, affirming the supremacy of lineage.

Today *Drukpa* school is the state religion in small Himalayan Kingdom.

In 1624, the fifth *Gyalwang Drukpa* Pagsam Wangpo satisfies the request of Ladakh's King — Sengye Namgyal — of a spiritual guide, sending in the country Taktsang Repa.

He ultimates, six days after, the building of Hemis' monastery, founding the *Sangha* (monastic community), becoming the main, wise reference of royal family and the Ladakhi people.

Within *Drukpa* school there is the belief that, since then, following incarnations of Taktsang Repa has been Ladakhi's Kings *gurus*.

Our story, then, brings us again to Hemis which had a crucial role for chronicles of Jesus' stay in India.

Why, then, I'm on *Druk Amitabha Mountain*?

Because in Ladakh, at Hemis, they recommend this place in Nepal as the one where actual *Gyalwang Drukpa* usually lives.

Only he can provide the necessary permission to look for the manuscripts that may still be in Hemis.

In the next chapter I'm going to share my experiences in Ladakh, going back a little in time and moving in the space while not forgetting the intrinsic value of the journey itself.

Ladakh (August 2014)

It was a journey I had been planning for several years.

I decided to visit Leh, the capital of Ladakh, an autonomous "state within a state" (Ladakh is officially part of Jammu and Kashmir state).

After arriving from Delhi I immediately began experiencing Acute Mountain Disease (AMD).

I settle in one room of a simple guest house in Changspa, the most touristic area of town, offering plenty of expensive, upmarket places.

But the guest house is ideal to stay for a few days while acclimatising to the altitude and its effects (the AMD).

In the following days, I visit "the old town", a much more interesting place. Indeed, I soon move there.

It has the advantage of being closer to the bus station, which I would like to use for visiting several places.

The new guest house is for experienced travellers. It has a wide courtyard and, in one corner, a long table. This, like everything else here, including the unstable chairs, is in a poor state, although it is perfect for socialising in the evening. Here the guests spend time together, drinking beer or local liquors, smoking, chatting and sharing mostly travel stories. It is like being back in the seventies, with cheap travels in Asia and nomadic, adventurous lifestyles. It is the ideal place to travel from, leaving heavy baggage behind.

And then, the *adhān* from a nearby Mosque makes impossible, for a Westerner, to forget he is "somewhere else".

I leave more than one time, just with basic things, leaving my baggage, money and laptop safe in my room, in Leh, without knowing exactly when I would return, choosing whether or not to sleep out of town according to the flow of events.

Ladakh is archaic and remote. It is sometimes difficult to use the internet, telephone cards are useless and it seems that nobody has the patience to follow the necessary procedures to get local ones.

It is easy to meet interesting people, especially on government bus; travellers of other times (maybe because the place is a pre-modern one).

With them I've sometimes scheduled vague appointments — without disposing of current, efficient communicative facilities — that were missed, leaving space and time for new encounters and new tales.

Everything happens in the harsh yet welcoming frame of an almost desert, high mountain environment. The cultural context is Tibetan with a strong Muslim minority (mostly Kashmiri).

The monasteries overlook small, humble villages.

The Indus river and its tributaries flow, shallow on their river-beds. The vegetation mottles a vaguely lunar landscape of irregular altitudes and pinnacles. The air is mercilessly dry, and scant oxygen means that movements and frequent climbs are strenuous.

The first visit is to Thiksey (in fact it is unscheduled. I had planned to go elsewhere, but underestimated the chaos of the bus station). Here, it is possible to visit one of the finest Ladakhi monasteries, which rises with the village up the side of the mountain.

The stone block monastery-village is, sometimes, mazy, with short underpasses and tunnels.

In one of these I find a board of a monastic school, whose entrance overlooks the ravine. It is easy to imagine a system of wooden stairs giving access to the upper floor, above the gallery itself, where segments of ancestral knowledge would have been transmitted, for several centuries, to young monks.

I lose my way, suffering from shortage of oxygen. My mind is overwhelmed by the charm of the place and I have no hurry to get — or to know how to get — anywhere. To be there, in the gallery, next to the monastery school, is enough.

I do not hesitate to take a break and get my breath back.

A monk comes out from the school. He is a child, probably no more than eleven or twelve years old.

«Where are you going?», he asks me with unexpected authority.

«To the monastery», I answer, almost comically overawed by him.

I, a big man, cowed by a child, but you should have seen the glance, the dignity.

He was clearly a wise adult in a child's body.

I follow his directions, soon reaching the monastery, which is famous for a beautiful statue of the Maitreya Buddha.

Thiksey's monastery belongs to Gelugpa (or Geluk) school, that of the current Dalai Lama. It has an intimate library housing many manuscripts on rice paper, each meticulously protected between two small wooden boards and in cloths embroidered with mythical and doctrinal motifs.

The monastery's terrace overlooks the green stained valley where the Indus river, a trickle of water, flows. The wooden interiors are snug and hieratic. The monks are particularly affable.

I return to Leh in the evening, not wanting to stay anywhere else. On my return, I stop in Shey at a nunnery (a monastery for nuns) called Naropa Pothang. It belongs to the *Drukpa* school, the same, as we've seen, of Hemis' monastery.

During my time in Leh, I bought the book *Ladakh: A Land*

of Magical Monasteries, which mentions the manuscripts of Hemis, connecting it to the nunnery in Shey. It explains that to access the manuscripts it is necessary to obtain a special permit from the Head Lama. It is not clear whether he is the abbot of the monastery or the *Gyalwang Drukpa*.

I speak to someone in the nunnery reception, telling her that I would be going to Hemis and would like an appointment with the Head Lama (my online researches revealed that "fortunately" the monastery has no website or email address).

She tells me that the Head Lama is in Nepal (on the *Druk Amithaba Mountain* — then we're talking about *Gyalwang Drukpa* even if will emerge, later, the crucial role of Hemis' abbot —) and I can talk with his attendant of whom she gives me the name and the mobile number.

Hemis

The next day, I leave for Hemis. Again, at the bus station I face problems.
The place is quite remote. Indeed, the book *Ladakh: A Land of Magical Monasteries* advises visitors to go to the nearest town, Karu.

However, there are no buses to Karu either, so I decide to hitchhike. It's an effective option in Ladakh. I did this on the previous day when returning from Shey, tired of waiting for the bus or minivan.

It's not difficult to get a lift, because it's an opportunity for drivers to earn a little money. One guy stops with his nice Toyota jeep. He asks me for quite a high fare, but I have a good feeling. I accept his deal and he will take me directly to Hemis.

The monastery occupies a niche in the mountains. Secluded and almost impregnable, it has been used for centuries to preserve ancient and precious goods.

Firstly, I ignore the monastery choosing to visit the nearby Gotsangpa's hermitage. Gotsangpa was one of the first saints of the *Drukpa* tradition. He lived between 1189 and 1258, being the founder of *To Druk*: "High Drukpa."

"Got" means "vulture", tsang means "nest". In Tibet and Ladakh vultures have their nests in the highest mountain areas.

In one of these vulture's nests, a cave in Ladakh not far from the future monastery of Hemis, Gotsangpa spent years in meditation with the pledge: «You, the bird, the rock and I: the man. Until I realise the oneness of the three, I will not leave this spot»[20].

On Gotsangpa's cave, centuries later, a hermitage was built in his name. At more than four thousand metres above sea level, above this place are only the barren and rocky peaks of the mountains. Some visible peaks are snow-capped, but what is most fascinating is the quality of silence.

Some verses come to mind of Shanti Deva, as meticulously reported by Coomaraswamy:

«Fain would I dwell in some deserted sanctuary, beneath a tree or in caves, that I might walk without heed, looking never behind! Fain would I abide in nature's own spacious and lordless lands, a homeless wanderer, free of will, my sole wealth a clay bowl, my cloak profitless to robbers, fearless and careless of my body»[21].

---

[20] Tsering N., *The monasteries of Hemis, Chemde and Dagthag*, New Delhi, p. 7.
[21] Ananda K. Coomaraswamy, *Buddha and the Gospel of Buddhism*, op. cit., p. 322.

Arriving at the hermitage, I reach Gotsangpa's cave. It is difficult to describe how rarefaction and the silence of the place saturates everything: the opening of a door, the creaking of the wooden planks under foot, the smile of the young monk who spontaneously leads me. In the back of the cave there are, in a shrine, some statues of Buddha and Padmasambhava[22].

A guy is meditating sitting on the floor.

The monk makes me touch the low ceiling of the cave. It exudes moisture.

In winter time, at minus thirty degrees, the place is probably freezing.

I sit beside the guy who meditates with open and welcoming palms resting on his knees. A monk sits in front of us, behind ritual bells, a large circular drum — in vertical position on wooden support — and a small table with a Tibetan manuscript.

After a few minutes a puja (celebration) begins.

The monk beats the drum repeatedly with a wooden rod.

He reads the contents of the manuscript following the rhythm of the drum.

Sometimes he takes a break, playing a typical Tibetan trumpet, then again, he beats the drum rapidly while reading the manuscript.

Again Shanti Deva:

---

[22]«Padma Sambhava was an 8th century Indian Buddhist sage and Tantric magician, who was invited to Tibet by Santarakshita, an Indian Buddhist master. With his great spiritual power, he created the conditions for the propagation of the teachings of Vajrayana Buddhism in this world.
[...]
In Sanskrit Padma means lotus flore and Sambhava means born from. In Tibet and Ladakh, Padma Sambhavaisalso known as Guru Rimpoche».
In: Gibbons Bob-Sian Pritchard Jones, *Ladakh land of magical monasteries*, Pilgrims Publishing, Varanasi, 2006, p. 25.

«Fain would I go to my home the graveyard, and compare with other skeletons my own frail body, for this my body will become so foul that the very jackals will not approach it because of its stench. The bony members born with this corporeal frame will fall asunder from it, much more so my friends. Alone man is born, alone he dies; no other has a share in his sorrows. What avail friends, but to bar his way? As a wayfarer takes a brief lodging, so he that is travelling through the way of existence finds in each birth but a passing rest»[23].

Again a sound of Tibetan trumpet, again some passages to be read, the drum to be beaten, and then the cave becomes totally silent.

I open my eyes, discovering a small mouse moving among holy paraphernalia.

I leave the cave for the hermitage's terrace.

The guy who was meditating beside me is also there. He looks at me, friendly and smiling.

«I saw you coming up», he starts.

«I saw you as well», I answer, «ahead of me, on the mountain's stairs, to climb has been exhausting!».

«Even for me», he says, «you've been stimulating, I didn't want you to join me because I was too tired».

«You also; I didn't want you — once in the hermitage — to think: that lazy guy has not been able to climb!».

We laugh. His name is Miro, a Slovak, doing a long journey in India and Nepal to think about his future. He has left his job. He's not engaged and doesn't know if he wants a "normal" kind of life.

We reach another part of the hermitage where another puja is in progress. Every sound is amplified by a slight rumble in

---

[23]Ananda K. Coomaraswamy, *Buddha and the Gospel of Buddhism*, op. cit., p. 322.

the "lunar" silence of the place. They offer us, several times, some butter tea.

I would like to remain for the night, to lose the sense of time, of plans. I would like to stay here and absorb everything, without the need to return anywhere, being able to lose the whole idea of return.

I will ask a monk if it is possible to stay here for the night without any prior reservation.

Miro, when the *puja* is finished, encourages me: «I already came here, yesterday. A young monk asked if I wanted to stay for the night», but he's more concerned about food.

The monks are not so welcoming. Most of them are old, probably living in the hermitage for a long time and never leaving. How could they? The climb to get here has worn down one young guy, Miro who is 32, and one almost as young…me. There is no other way to get here. We decide to ask for some food.

«Lunch is ready», a monk tells us.

We follow him on other stairways, on the ridge of the mountain, again climbing, with our faces shredded by arid wind. We arrive at one small, stony building: the hermitage canteen. Outside, on a small wall, are three cauldrons.

Many monks have arrived before us, but none fills his dish till we hear the sound of a bell.

Miro and I, according to my knowledge of monastic rules, must wait our turn until the last monk has taken his food. Then, the monk who has been leading us indicates a small tank of water, ordering us to wash our hands. We obey.

I would like to see inside the canteen, but I simply ask: «Do we eat here?», indicating the inside.

«No!», answers the monk, «wait!». Meanwhile, the cauldrons disappeared.

The wind from snow-capped peaks, starts to become frosty.

The monk entered the canteen and has now returned with two dishes of rice and boiled vegetables.

He gives us the dishes and returns inside the canteen.

Miro and I look at each other slightly confused. He didn't even give us a fork!

«Let's sit there», I propose, indicating a low wall.

We eat the rice and tasteless vegetables with our hands. It is almost an effort to speak as we absorb such a wonderfully harsh environment. We speak a few words about Italy, a few about Slovakia and a few about our lives, Ladakh, and the reasons for being on that mountain, almost unwanted by surly monk-hermits.

After our meagre meal we wash our dishes. The monk who led us to the canteen is passing nearby.

I don't think there is any chance to be welcomed for the night, but I ask him anyway.

The answer is very direct: «No!».

I say to Miro: «I will not go back to Leh, today, but will rent a room in the monastery's guest house».

«I'm staying with a family in the village. I pitched my tent in their land», says Miro.

«Wow!», I answer, «the home-stay would be the best option!».

We start walking in the direction of the Hemis monastery and village, leaving the hermitage behind us.

Unlike Thiksey, Hemis' village is not combined in the same block as the monastery; it has developed independently in a niche of the valley below.

It is rather secluded, composed of around twenty stone houses beside a small stream. Just houses, no shops, but a fountain with an iron lever and a few dogs wandering around.

We go to the house where Miro is hosted, slightly outside the village. The owners are not there.

We head towards the stream, talking with some locals.

People look at us in a neutral manner, with neither curiosity nor hostility.

«I'm looking for a room», I publicly say, «has someone a room to rent for this night?».

Fortunately, Ladakhi have a good knowledge of English.

A girl brings me to her house, twenty metres from the stream, but isolated from the others. She shows me a decent room, but I'm not happy with the price. It is too high and, despite understanding the need for locals to earn money from foreigners, I prefer to be hosted by more simple people. I thank her and go back to the stream.

Miro looks at me quizzically.

«Don't worry», I make him understand.

I cross the stream and begin walking through the alleys of the village. A man is walking in the opposite direction, in an alley so narrow that we can barely pass each other.

I greet him and ask directly: «I need a room, could you please help me?».

He has two vaguely blue eyes on a face dried by the Himalayan wind and furrowed by wrinkles. His reactions are slow and placid, in keeping with the vibe of the place.

«I can show you the room we use for our relatives, if for you it is okay…».

«Great», I answer, «let's see it!».

The room is very nice, better than the former I saw. It is a kind of studio with a kitchen. Several mattresses and pillows at the sides of the room mark its perimeter.

On each mattress there are, neatly folded, sheets and blankets. Beside each mattress there is a small, carved table with images of dragons (*drukpa*).

«How much money I can give you to sleep one night here?» I ask.

He's a little confused and doesn't answer; he is the person I was looking for; a pure local who has never thought to profit from a visiting foreigner.

I insist: «How may I reciprocate your politeness? I'd like to pay for the disturbance».

«Give me what you want», he answers.

We agree to a reasonable amount and I tell him about Miro. He's also welcome him and we can also have dinner.

I join Miro and he's amazed by my enthusiasm. He wants to see the room.

The room, which is pretty, simple, functional and clean, pleases him.

The house, in general, is really disarming, with a small vegetable garden, some clothes hanging to dry and a bundled-up baby in the arms of a toothless grandmother.

And then there is our host: blue-eyed, calm and vital, attentive and kindly, yet suggesting a hard life.

«I will dismantle the tent and join you», says Miro.

«Alright», I answer, «I propose that we pay extra to have dinner with them».

«Sure», answers Miro.

Soon we're all in the kitchen of the house, sitting on mattresses marking the perimeter of the room.

Our hosts switch the television on and then soon switch it off.

The wife of our host is quietly busy cooking. Soon, the food is ready and served in abundance.

There are no real conversations, except for short moments, but the company is pleasant, the light very soft and we enjoy this kind of intimacy.

The following day, sitting on the low wall of the house, looking at the simple vegetable garden and drinking our tea, Miro offers some deep reflections: «I think I'd like to live as they're doing», he says.

Indeed, in that simplicity there is nothing, except the *essentials*!

I am also inclined to these kinds of reflections and every day I am more attracted by a "way out from the world."

After a few days, in fact, I am there again, but this time alone.

Miro bought a 1988 Enfield motorbike in Manali[24], thinking to re-sell it upon leaving India.

That morning we sipped tea looking at the vegetable garden used for the subsistence of our welcoming Ladakhi family. Then we returned to Leh on his Enfield, with our faces dried up by the wind, enjoying landscapes of irregular peaks and humble villages

We vaguely planned to travel together, in the evening, to a meeting. However, the difficulties of language and communication discouraged us, so we opted for a final farewell.

To salute Miro has been to salute a genuine companion of research. Again, words by Coomaraswamy's book can help to express what is probably the illusory nature of each separation:

«Thou goest thine, and I go mine—
Many ways we wend
Many days and, many ways,
Ending in one end.

Many a wrong, and its curing song
Many a word, and many an inn:
Room to roam, but only one home
For all the world to win».[25]

---

[24]A famous mountain place in Indian state of Himachal Pradesh.
[25]Ananda Coomaraswamy, *Buddha and the Gospel of Buddhism*, op. cit., p. 194.

Again to Hemis

The return to Leh, after the experience in the hermitage and the night in the village, has been quite frustrating.

After an evening of chat, drinking poor Indian whiskey, smoking my pipe and listening the stories of my neighbour, Derek, about Eelam[26] — whose palms were largely beheaded by a never ending and merciless war and where everything expressed a clear feeling of death — I cannot avoid planning a new visit to the Ladakhi family.

And then, if it is true that the journey is more important than the destination, it is even important to avoid excessive distractions, missing the chance to reach it.

My first visit to Hemis brought results. I visited the famous monastery's museum, talking with the person in charge, Jigme, and, as already noted, the personal secretary of the Head Lama.

I asked about the manuscripts and the possibility of getting a meeting with the only person who can authorise their viewing.

Jigme confirms what I read in the booklet *The Monasteries of Hemis, Chedme and Dagthag*, on sale in museum's shop: the manuscripts are held in a secret room called, by locals, *dzodnag*.

Only the Abbot of Hemis, His Holiness Taktsang Rinpoche, can break the room's seals, enabling the access to the manuscripts.

However, Taktsang Rinpoche lives in Lhasa, and in the same booklet it is written that he has no objection to access being granted to sincere researchers. Indeed, he has officially

---

[26]Area in North of Sri Lanka mostly populated by Tamil who unsuccessfully attempted, through a long civil war, to get independence.

requested that they to be helped in the search for old documents.

However, somebody joined the monastery with a letter written by the Abbot but, still, he could not see the manuscripts.

The booklet reports that the only entrance to *dzodnag* is by the private room of the Abbot.

After learning all of this, I consult Jigme, hoping for more information. As with other monks I have talked with, Jigme says that nobody knows where the manuscripts are and that even the location of *dzodnag* is a mystery.

I reach the house of the Ladakhi family who previously hosted me and Miro. I will spend a couple of nights there.

On this second visit I become more aware of the quiet nature of the people and their equally quiet environment, reminiscent of the Arctic.

The lower slopes feature a scattering of trees and along the mountain ridges there is limited vegetation with a scattering of bushes. This gives way to bare ground with a moss or lichen-like cover.

The animals are silent, too, although from time to time this is broken by the croaking of a bird.

The same silence pervades the Spartans and simple interiors.

I begin some bare conversation, facilitated by my hosts' minimal knowledge of English and my basics of Hindi.

Their mother tongue, however, is Ladakhi, similar to Tibetan. But our limited conversations are not caused by language differences.

It is merely their way to use few and simple words.

I am always the only one trying to lead the conversation, but they answer in a gentle, even sweet manner, then again become silent.

Therefore, during my stay, we share a silence without any embarrassment, in tune with the silent environment.

The words, useless, roll down the ridges of consciousness, as stones sink in a river. Then it is possible to feel the fulness of the golden silence, oldest of the old expressions of creation.

I clearly feel whatever is said is awkward and I try to be a simple witness of these moments. And, after the words, the thoughts start falling too, along the creaking of an old-wooden door and, finally, the specious Descartes' assumption: «I think therefore I am» reverses, giving way to a more reliable: «I am therefore I am».

This could really neutralise the arrogance of the West, that is paving the way to its prophesied decline[27].

During my short stay in the village of Hemis, I get to know the grandson of the householder. He is around sixteen and became a monk when he was nine. He's now studying in a monastic school.

I tell him the main purpose of my visit. He also does not know anything about the *dzodnag* and tells me the Abbot of Hemis' monastery is in Tibet. He gives me a card with the image of Taktsang Rinpoche beside the *Gyalwang Drukpa* who lives in Nepal.

I think I will be forced to visit that country to get a new visa for India. Before the challenge of visiting Tibet (mostly its monasteries and monks) I can focus on a more simple stay at the head-lineage's monastery, trying to progress with the search.

---

[27]Here there is a reference to a book, published in 1918, with a probable prophetic title: *The decline of the West*, by Oswald Spengler.

***

My stay, in October 2014, on *Druk Amitabha Mountain* will be, as mentioned, very intense.

It will be preceded by an email that will get a quick but hazy answer.

I will remain around ten days in a Nepali nunnery, soliciting an interview with the *Gyalwang Drukpa*.

I will have just a couple of meetings with a nun of his staff who will give me no guarantee of a meeting with His Holiness.

«He's constantly busy», she will tell me more than once. «I will do my best but it will be difficult, for you, to meet him».

She will take notes about the book I am writing asking why I decided to do it.

During the second meeting she will ask me explicitly: «Do you want to write this book to become famous or for other reasons?».

«I appreciate this question», I reply, «I think it is important to reduce the gap between East and West, if we are able to demonstrate we have a crucial figure as Jesus in common we could make important steps forward…and, then, Christianity really needs a deep regeneration, to better contribute to the formation of a new, universal man!».

She is also satisfied with my answer, but it is approaching the time of an important pilgrimage, led by His Holiness, in India, in historical places of the first Buddhism: the *Pad Yatra*.

Then, *Gyalwang Drukpa* will leave the quiet of the Nepali mountain a few days before me, followed by the majority of the nuns.

With a new visa on my passport, I will return to Varanasi, with some more references about *Drukpa* school and, in particular, one of its offices specifically dedicated to publications, in India.

***

Before leaving Hemis I cautiously ask to the young monk if he is happy (as I feel) with his condition and if he has sometimes an even slight desire for a more mundane life.

He answers in a lapidary way: «We (monks) are different!». He then reverts to his natural condition of silence.

We remain silent for few minutes then he gets up and, taking his leave in an essential but affable way, he leaves me alone in the guest room, watching the vanishing of my thoughts in the golden silence of that — unforgettable — place.

Srinagar, five years later
(Beginning of September 2014)

After the intense journey in Ladakh I start the return trip to to Srinagar. From Kargil, an almost entirely Muslim town at border between Ladakh and Kashmir, we buy a lift on a jeep with two aged yet sprightly British women.

There is the option of a night bus to Srinagar but the journey should be done during the day due to the amazing beauty of the landscapes. We leave immediately after lunch. We cross humid mountain lands, on muddy roads on the edge of the precipice.

Those mountains are a never-ending pasture for herds of leathery and almost wild sheep, led by shepherds who are also forged by the tough environment.

The shepherds often belong to an ethnic minority probably of Afghan origin. Somebody claims they could be — at least some of them — heirs of Alexander the Great's army because of their features often bearing a resemblance to those from Greece. They often live in tents lashed by the wind and covered with moisture, not far from streams.

Tents are sometimes isolated, far from other small and precarious human settlings. Other times they are aggregated in nomadic camps.

We will travel under what seems like neverending rain. We return to Srinagar by nightfall and, the day after, I am once again in the house of Professor Hassnain.

He is glad to see me again and he signs a reference letter which will be useful for my research.

I tell him about my stay in Ladakh, about *dzodnag* and the need to be received by the Abbot of Hemis' monastery or by

Gyalwang Drukpa. We reflect it should be possible to find some other copies of manuscripts Notovitch wrote about, Tibetan translation from Pali originals, in other monasteries or, maybe, in private collections.

However now, during my stay in Srinagar, it is time to follow another path.

We plan another visit to the *Rozabal* and, then, to *Ahmadiyya Muslim Community*.

Everything strictly under the rain (after a few days Kashmir will suffer one of the worst floods of last decades, thanks to God, I was been able to avoid it, coincidently leaving a couple of days before the disaster).

I undertake an interview of the shrine's guardian. A student of Professor Hassnain supports me with the language difference.

The guardian refutes beyond any doubt that Yuzu Asaph was Jesus, claiming, instead, he was a mysterious — but certainly Islamic — figure.

The *Ahmadiyya Muslim Community* is much more welcoming. From the big courtyard of its property, I soon enter in to one of the private rooms. It is particularly net and clean, with a sweet perfume, typical of many Muslim interiors.

A couple of quite young men amazingly welcome me with a hug each.

When I tell them the reason of my visit they become even more polite with me.

They propose to visit their library where I can take pictures of several documents supporting the hypothesis of Jesus' long stay in India.

At the entrance of the library, a painting of a rough map shows the route he is proposed to have travelled from Palestine to India, crossing the territories of modern day Syria, Iraq, Iran, Afghanistan and Pakistan.

«You have arrived in the right place», Dr. Aijaz, a surgeon and member of Community tells me, «we are the most interested in Jesus' stay in India and we are at your disposal!».

Indeed, most of the material available in the library (for examples photocopies of texts and documents exposed in display cases) is related to this topic at hand.

«When do you intend to leave?», Aijaz asks me.

«I have to take the plane tomorrow», I answer.

«Why don't you change the date of flight? You can take a train for Amritsar and, then, you can continue to Qadian which is our Indian headquarters. You can be hosted for free and you can use our main library, in case you will need assistance, somebody will help you», he tells me.

I thank him but I prefer to proceed step by step.

I need to go back to Varanasi but I promise to Aijaz to contact him soon to organize my stay in Qadian.

It is difficult, for me, to leave these friendly people, going back to my hotel, again under a merciless downpour of rain.

The day after, my flight will be delayed, because of the terrible weather conditions.

Back in Varanasi, I soon know about tragic inundations in Kashmir and groups of Kashmiri irredentists refusing the first aid interventions of New Delhi's army. I will send one copy of *The second coming of Christ*, by Paramahansa Yogananda and one of *Swami Abhedananda's Journey to Kashmir and Tibet* — very difficult to find outside *Ramakrishna Mission*'s seats (fortunately one of them has a good bookshop in Varanasi) — to Professor Hassnain.

The books too will arrive with a delay but they will make the Professor very happy.

We will talk some time later and he will reassure me about his good health. He has survived the inundations, after so many dangers, living many years in a place Bill Clinton defined, in 2002, "the most risky in the world".

Varanasi (November-13 December 2014)

I leave Nepal at the end of October for a pleasant stay, of fourty days, in Varanasi. I put in order all the collected material to date and I proceed in my research, both reading and writing.

I will soon be back on the road, this time going to Qadian.

During my stay in Varanasi I list, in chronological order, the most important events and books about the hypothetical stay of Jesus in India, according to the material I have collected online, in libraries and bookshops and, again, out in the field:

1849 It is published, in Leipzig (Germany), a very old document where one Essene contemporary of Jesus pro-poses "the true life and death of Rabbi". The document has been translated, in French, in 1863 and, ten years later, in English with the title: *Crucifixion by an eye witness*. Another translation in English appeared in 1907.

1894 Nicholas Notovitch publishes in Paris, with Paul Ollendorff Editeurs, *La Vie inconnue de Jésus Christ*, translated into English (by Alexina Loranger) the same year and published by Indo-American Book Company in Chicago.

1899 Hadhrat Mirzā Ghulām Ahmad ends *Jesus in India*, several sections of which will be published in the *Review of Religions*[28] in 1902/1903.

---

[28]«The Review of Religions, in print since 1902, is one of the longest-running comparative religious magazines.

The book will be published, posthumous, in 1908, in Urdu language. It will be translated into English in 1944;

1908 First edition of *The Aquarian Gospel of Jesus Christ*, by American Protestant minister Levi H. Dowling (1844-1911). The book has an esoteric approach, reporting Jesus' travels and periods of life in India, Tibet, Persia, Egypt and Greece;

1922 Travel of Swami Abhedananda (1866-1939)[29] in Kashmir and Tibet even with deliberate purpose to search manuscripts found by Notovitch in Hemis' monastery.
To the experience on the field will follow the publication — in Bengali in 1929 and in English in 1987 — of the book *Swami Abhedananda's journey to Kashmir and Tibet;*

1929 Publication of books *Altai-Himalaya* and *Heart of Asia*, by Russian painter and writer Nicholas Roerich (1874-1947), where it is mentioned the rich oral tradition about Jesus' stay in Kashmir and in Himalayan territories. Between 1923 and 1928 Roerich has leaded one expedition in several areas of India, Tibet, Sikkim, Turkestan and Mongolia (Altai).
Reports about that — with the mention of Roerich's hypothesis of Jesus' stay in India — appeared on *New York Times* (27th May 1926) and other magazines;

1956 Publication of *Jesus in heaven on earth*, by Ahmad Al Haj Khwaja Nazir. It is a book written in a very accurate and

---

The objective of the magazine is to present the teachings of Islam, reflecting its rational, harmonious and inspiring nature. It also brings together articles and viewpoints on different religions and seeks to make discussions on religion and religious philosophy accessible to a wider readership». In: *www.reviewofreligions.org*
[29]Vicepresident of *Ramakrishna Math and Mission* between 1921 and 1924. He travelled in US, teaching Vedanta, between 1897 and 1921.

professional way. Nowadays it is difficult to find it in paper format.
It is possible to buy it on line or to download the pdf for free.

1963 First edition of *The serpent of paradise, the story of an Indian pilgrimage*, by Miguel Serrano, where hypothesis of "Indian years of Jesus" is presented with plenty of details;

1973 First edition of *Christ in Kashmir*, by Aziz Kashmiri, an important text about "Indian years of Jesus", today almost unobtainable;

1973 First edition of O.M. Burke's *Among the dervishes* where it is reported a period Jesus spent in Afghanistan and it is presented quite accurately a Christian community (*The Followers of Jesus*) which fully accepts the authenticity of "Indian history" of Palestinian Master;

1974 Realization of Richard Bock's movie *The lost years of Jesus*; it is available on You Tube, offering fascinating images of India at the beginning of the seventies.

1983 Publication of *Jesus lived in India*, by Holger Kersten;

1988 Publication of *The Fifth Gospel*, by Professor Maria Fida Hassnain and Dahan Levi;

1985 Publication of *The Rajneesh Bible*, where it is supported the thesis of Jesus' stay in India before and after crucifixion;

1991 Publication of excellent book, by Paul Pappas: *Jesus tomb in India, the debate on his death and resurrection*;

1994 Publication of *The lost years of Jesus*, by Elizabeth Clare Prophet;

1995 Publication of *The original Jesus*, by Holger Kersten and Elmar R. Gruber.
The book analyses many parallelisms between Christianity and Buddhism, proposing a clear influence by the second on the first;

1995 Publication of *The Jesus Conspiracy*, by Holger Kersten and Elmar R. Gruber.
The book focuses on scientific studies about Turin Shroud that would confirm the hypothesis Jesus survived to crucifixion;

2003 Realization of BBC documentary *Jesus in India/Did Jesus die?* It is available on You Tube, in integral version and in a couple of partial versions with different titles for instance: *Was Jesus a Buddhist monk?* These and other documentaries, as well as other documents, are easily available in facebook page **Jesus in India?** and in **Viverealtrimenti You Tube channel;**

2004 Publication of *The second coming of Christ*, with scripts by ParamahansaYogananda, where are deeply considered the "Indian years" of Jesus;

2006 Realization of documentary *The Unknown Story of the Messiah*, by Subhrajit Mitra. It has been proposed to fifteen festivals, included Cannes' one;

2006 Publication of Swami Sivananda's *Life and teachings of Lord Jesus* where the hypothesis of Jesus' stay in India has been positively considered;

2007 Publication, in US, of thriller *The Rozabal Line*, by Indian writer Ashwin Sanghi, considered the "Indian Dan Brown". The book has been published, the following year, in India, with big success of public and critic, becoming soon a *bestseller*. How it is possible to guess from the title, the book is based on the hypothesis of "Indian years" of Jesus;

2009 Realization of Paul Davis' movie *Jesus in India*;

2009 Publication, in London, of Alan Jacobs' book *When Jesus lived in India;*

2010 Realization of documentary *The Rozabal shrine of Srinagar*.
Written and directed by Yashendra, it has been produced by the Film Division of the Government of India.

According to this list, it is quite evident the issue of Indian years of Jesus has been considered — in depth — by several authors, directors, etc.

I think it is interesting the heterogeneity of proposed material, produced by Kashmiri, Indian, European and American authors.

In last twenty years reaserches diversified and, often, specialized.

The interest for the topic of this book, then, has not remained confined to the period shortly followed the books of pioneers Notovitch and Mirzā Ghulām Ahmad. Many others have been deeply inspired by them, going on with the research.

In following pages I will give more details about some mentioned documents, starting with *Crucifixion by an eye witness*.

According to what has been asserted by the researchers appearing in the documentary *The Unknown Story of the Messiah*, some important Indian institutions — as Kolkata's *Asiatic Society* — start to be interested in the topic of "Indian years" of Jesus.

I invite again the readers to visit regularly facebook page ***Jesus in India?*** to be constantly updated.

The Crucifixion, By An Eye-Witness

In 1849, in Leipzig, a very ancient document was published.

This document claimed to be from a high ranking member of the Essene Order, a contemporary of Jesus.

In the document the Essene member narrates to a Therapeut of Alexandria the "true story" surrounding the life and death of the "Rabbi", referring to Jesus Christ.

The original, written on large sheets of parchment, was discovered — in an abandoned library of a ruined convent which hosted Greek monks from Athos mountain — in Alexandria (Egypt).

Following archaeological research the time period of this document was established as between the first century B.C. and the first century A.D. The manuscript were confirmed to have been documented as property of the Essenes. It claims to have been written "seven Easters" after Jesus' crucifixion in Jerusalem.

The publication of the document by a Rosicrucians group — with the title *The Crucifixion, By An Eye-Witness* — created a lot of noise for several reasons: it confirmed Jesus was a member of Essene's order and offered interesting details about his life. The most important detail, according to this document, is that he did not die on the cross but was deposed still alive, in a kind of semi-conscious state appearing as death.

Because of this Joseph of Arimathea and Nicodemus — Essenes of the highest degree — had been able to avoid the fracture of Jesus' legs (practice known as *crurifragium*, whose purpose was to hasten the death of those on the cross through choking) and, then, to transfer him in one of their convents where he, later, died.

The Crucifixion, By An Eye-Witness does not contribute to the hypothesis of Jesus' stay in India while it does strongly support the more widespread one of his survival from the ordeal of crucifixion.

In fact, the death of Jesus on the cross has been, since the beginning, a matter of skepticism for many people for several reasons, which will be examined in the course of this text.

We can start by mentioning one of the strongest arguments, which is focused on limited duration — as it is clear from the Gospels — Jesus remained on the cross (three to six hours), generally considered insufficient to cause death.

Joseph of Arimathea and Nicodemus — as Essenes (again: according to the document in analysis) — were experts in the medical practice, knowing how to revive a body in apparent death, if the same body was received in time: after just a few hours on the cross.

Then, they were successful in preventing the *crurifragium* (a fate suffered by the two thieves crucified to Jesus' right and to his left), the fracture of Jesus' legs and they could see, from the wound to the side by the spear of Longinus, the body was still alive.

Indeed there was a flow of blood and water[31] and the Essenes knew that if the body was really dead then from this wound "nothing but a few drops of thickened blood"[32] would have flowed out.

---

[31] «[…]One of the soldiers pierced His side with a spear, and immediately blood and water came out» (John: 19,34.)
[32] *The Crucifixion, By An Eye-Witness*, Indo-American Book Co, Chicago, 1915, pp. 71-72.

Another interesting passage from *The Crucifixion, By An Eye-Witness* offers an alternative version of what happened near the tomb shortly after Jesus was laid to rest there.

The Gospel of Matthew reports a great earthquake and the appearance of an angel, descended from heaven, to overturn the stone closing access to the grave and sitting on it:

«And the guards shook for fear of him, and became like dead men» (Mt 28,4).

In the version of the old paper published for the first time in Leipzig, the Angel was none other than a young Essene member who «went to the grave in obedience to the order of the Brotherhood, dressed in the white robe of the fourth degree white tunic»[33]:

«When the timid servants of the high priest[34] saw the white-robed Brother on the mountain slowly approaching, and partially obscured by the morning mist, they were seized with a great fear,

---

[33]*Ivi*, pp. 77-78.

[34]In the version of *The Crucifixion, By An Eye-Witness* instead of Roman soldiers guarding the tomb, there were a number of armed servants of high-priest Caiaphas who had a strong suspect something was going on between Joseph of Arimathea and the Galileans, in support of Jesus' innovative perspectives:

«And so it was that Caiaphas anticipated secret plans between the rich Joseph and the Galileans, and knowing that they intended to embalm the body, he hoped there to catch them, as the idea had occurred to him that Joseph and Pilate were plotting against the Jews.

Fear of this caused him great anxiety, and for this reason he hoped to discover some secret means of accusing Joseph and having him thrown into prison. He betrayed this fact himself by sending late in the night a number of his armed servants to an obscure valley close by the grotto in which lay the body of Jesus. Some distance from them was stationed a detachment of the temple guard, to assist the servants of the high-priest, if necessary.

But the rumor has told you that this guard were Roman soldiers, which was not the case. The high-priest even distrusted Pilate». (*Ivi*, p. 76)

and they thought that an angel was descending from the mountain»[35].

The text continues that after he recovered, Jesus wanted to see his disciples in Galilee but, once in Emmaus, he decided to travel immediately to Jerusalem, where he met them. Not long after this, he retired to an Essene monastery near the Dead Sea, upon whose shores he was later buried.

The Crucifixion, By An Eye-Witness has been scrupulously studied and highly considered by important scholars in Germany: D.E. Strauss, Arnold Ruge, Bruno Bauer, Ludwig Feuerbach, etc.

L.S. Fugairon & J.Bricaud, prominent members of Universal Gnostic Church, claim the tale contained in *The Crucifixion, By An Eye-Witness* is in tune with most secret gnostic traditions and, mostly, with the *Pistis Sophia*[36].

However, in the *Pistis Sophia* Jesus is reported to have spent eleven years with his pupils but, according Fugairon and Bricaud, this time period could be considered from an esoteric perspective, and thus be figurative.

In general, the most important aspect of *The Crucifixion, By An Eye-Witness* is a less sensationalistic and fantastic version of the last events of Jesus' life.

Indeed, he does not resurrect, he just survives the crucifixion, due to the planning and intervention by his Essene brothers.

---

[35] *The Crucifixion, By An Eye-Witness*, op. cit., p. 78.
[36] «A 3rd-cent. Egyptian work which purports to record instruction given by Christ to certain disciples at the end of a twelve-year sojourn on earth after the Resurrection. It relates the salvation of the personified 'Pistis Sophia' (i.e.'Faith-Wisdom') from a demon named 'Self-Will'».

In: *www.oxfordindex.oup.com*

No angel sits in front of an empty tomb, just a young Essene who scares the guards, even because a recent earthquake and their probable emotional and psychological fragility.

Indeed they were standing guard over the corpse of a uncommon person; the probable superstitions of that time could have played a prominent role in that.

The epilogue of eye witness' tale is sober and discreet as well: after he has instructed his pupils, Jesus retires and — in understandable suffering physical conditions because of the ordeal of crucifixion — does not survive for long. Then, he is secretly buried on the shores of the Dead Sea.

We have presented here a version of final part of Jesus' life which today, in a secularized and disillusioned West, is easily plausible, unlike what we could define "the mythicisation of Jesus' story".

We should, however, consider that mythicisation was been necessary, at the dawn of Christianity, to persuade and convert heterogeneous and mostly illiterate masses.

Finally, it is important to highlight that each rational consideration cannot go beyond faith issues, which, of course, cannot be argued in this book.

Nicholas Notovitch and the disappeared manuscripts

Nicholas Notovitch[37] was born in Crimea in 1858 as the second son of a Rabbi. When he became an adult, he converted to Orthodox Christianity as he publicly admitted in French journal *La Paix*.

After the Turkish War (1877-1878), he writes in the Preface of *The unknown life of Jesus Christ*, he made several trips to Asia, arriving in 1887 in India.

After Kashmir he visited Ladakh, intending to go back to Russia by way of Kara-korum and Chinese Turkestan.

In a Ladakhi Buddhist monastery, in Mulbekh, he was informed about the existence of very ancient manuscripts reporting a long journey of Jesus in India during the years that the Gospels are silent about.

Shortly after this he visited the Hemis monastery, again in Ladakh, where some copies of manuscripts "about the Indian years of Jesus" were said to be stored and preserved.

After a first, short and fruitless stay in the monastery, Notovitch was forced to stay longer because of an unfortunate fall not far from the monastery resulting in him breaking one of his legs.

In this critical physical condition, he was hosted by the monks for a period long enough to gain the trust of the chief lama, see the manuscripts, and have them translated with the vital cooperation of his interpreter.

Back in Europe, he decided to look for a publisher to make public his translation.

---

[37]It is possible to read a detailed biography of Nicholas Notovitch in the Appendix.

In the Preface of his book Notovitch writes:

«Mgr. Platon, the celebrated metropolitan of Kiev, thought that my discovery was of great importance. Nevertheless, he sought to dissuade me from publishing the memoirs, believing that their publication could only hurt me. "Why?" This the venerable prelate refused to tell me more explicitly. Nevertheless, since our conversation took place in Russia, where the censor would have put his veto upon such a work, I made up my mind to wait.
A year later, I found myself in Rome. I showed my manuscript to a cardinal very near to the Holy Father, who answered me literally in these words: "What good will do to print this? Nobody will attach to it any great importance and you will create a number of enemies. But, you are still very young! If it is a question of money which concerns you, I can ask for you a reward for your notes, a sum which will repay your expenditures and recompense you for your loss of time". Of course, I refused.
In Paris I spoke of my project to Cardinal Rotelli, whose acquaintance I had made in Constantinople. He, too, was opposed to having my work printed, under the pretext it would be premature. "The church", he added, "suffers already too much from the new current of atheistic ideas, and you will give a new food to the calumniators and detractors of the evangelical doctrine.
I tell you this in the interest of all the Christian churches".
Then I went to see M. Jules Simon. He found my matter very interesting and advised me to ask the opinion of M. Renan[38], as to the best way of publishing these memoirs.
The next day I was seated in the cabinet of the great philosopher. At the close of our conversation, M. Renan proposed that I should confide to him the memoirs in question, so that he might make to the Academy a report upon the discovery. [...]

---

[38]Ernest Renan (1823-1892) has been a French expert of Semitic languages and civilizations (philology), philosopher, historian, and writer. He authored the very popular *Life of Jesus* where Christ is depicted as heroic but not divine. Member of *Académie Française*, Renan has exerted a great influence on the culture of his time.

I thought myself sufficiently prepared to publish the translation of the chronicles, accompanying them with my notes, and, therefore, did not accept the very gracious offer he made to me».[39]

As already written, the book *La vie inconnue de Jesus Christ* had been published, in Paris, in 1894.

In its first section it is a pleasant travel book, with some modest hermeneutical and anthropological excursions.

The second section reports the translation of manuscripts and it is called *The life of Saint Issa, best of the sons of men.*

It starts mentioning the torture and death sentence of the "great and right Issa", proceeding with a long tale by merchants coming from Palestine, beginning with the mention of the enslaving of the Jews in Egypt, their exodus, the period of independence and prosperity till the Roman conquest.

Through this subjugation they held firm to their belief in their God.

«Soon after, a marvellous child was born in the land of Israel. God himself spoke, through the mouth of this child, of the miseries of the body and the grandeur of the soul»[40].

According to the tale in analysis, the "divine child", Issa, became soon famous, and Jews begun to think the "Eternal Spirit" was living within him.

When he was thirteen, the proper age for marrying, he left, secretly, his father's home, escaping from rich and noble householders competing to have him in their families.

He joined a merchants' caravans directed to a land known, at that time, as Sindh, «with the object of perfecting himself

---

[39] Nicholas Notovitch, *The Unknown Life of Jesus Christ*, Hachette India, Gurgaun, 2013, pp. IX-X.
[40] *Ivi*, p. 76.

in the knowledge of the word of God and the study of the laws of the great Buddhas»[41].

According to manuscripts found and translated by Notovitch, Issa entered in India from the West, crossing territories of actual Punjab and Rajastan where fervent Jains tried to make him stay with them.

In the same manuscripts it is written he went to Orissa to study with the "white priests of Brahma" in Puri at the *Jagannath Temple*, where he achieved important Vedic notions.

He lived for six years in several Indian holy towns, including Benares, giving his teachings to all, importantly including members of low castes.

He offered one perspective with peculiar Jews elements: monotheism, an iconoclastic attitude and an eschatology with clear apocalyptic veins. We can find some elements of the *Sermon on the Mount* and, more generally, of the *Decalogue* as well in his teachings reported in this text:

«The eternal Judge, the eternal Spirit, constitutes the only and indivisible soul of the universe, and it is this soul alone which creates, contains and vivifies all. He alone has willed and created. He alone has existed from eternity, and His existence will be without end; there is no one like unto Him either in the heavens or on the earth.
The great Creator has divided His power with no other being; far less with inanimate objects, as you have been taught to believe, for He alone is omnipotent and all-sufficient.
He willed, and the world was. By one divine thought, He reunited the waters and separated them from the dry land of the globe. He is the cause of the mysterious life of man, into whom He has breathed part of His divine Being.
And He has put under subjection to man, the lands, the waters, the beasts and everything which He created, and which He

---

[41]*Ivi*, p. 77.

himself preserves in immutable order, allotting to each its proper duration.
The anger of God will soon break forth upon man; for he has forgotten his Creator; he has filled His temples with abominations; and he adores a multitude of creatures which God has subordinated to him;
And to gain favor with images of stone and metal, he sacrifices human beings in whom dwells part of the Spirit of the Most High.
And he humiliates those who work in the sweat of their brows, to gain favor in the eyes of the idler who sit at a sumptuous table.
Those who deprive their brothers of divine happiness will themselves be deprived of it; and the Brahmins and the Kshatriyas [the dominant castes, in India, of "priests" and warriors] shall become the Sudras [servants] of the Sudras, with whom the Eternal will stay forever.
In the day of judgement the Sudras and the Vaisyas [traders] will be forgiven for that they knew not the light, while God will let loose his wrath upon those who arrogated his authority.
The Vaisyas and the Sudras were filled with great admiration, and asked Issa how they should pray, in order not to lose their hold upon the eternal life.
"Pray not to idols, for they cannot hear you; hearken not to the Vedas where the truth is altered; be humble and humiliate not your fellow man.
Help the poor, support the weak, do evil to none, cover not that which ye have not and which belongs toothers"»[42].

Of course, such a direct challenge to caste establishment soon caused strong reactions and a death sentence was decreed against the young prophet.

With the help of the *sudras* (members of low castes), Issa escaped from the territories of Puri, in Orissa Indian state, to settle in the lands where Buddha Shakyamuni was born (in

---

[42]*Ivi*, pp. 80-81.

actual districts of Terai, in the South of Nepal, bordering with actual Indian state of Uttar Pradesh).

In the native lands of the Buddha he learns the Pali language, studying Buddhist scriptures.

After a period of around six years, he starts to move back to the West, converting several pagans and idolaters to the law of the "Eternal Judge". He stops, for a while, in Persia, creating some problems for the local Zoroastrian priests.

When he is twenty nine he is back in Palestine where he finds his people heavily oppressed by Roman yoke. He starts to preach in towns and villages of his land, becoming very popular.

Many people spread rumours he wants to become the king of his people after a violent insurrection.

The rumours arrive to the Roman Governor Pontius Pilate who orders Issa to be arrested and tortured. The Jewish Rabbis ask to judge Issa in their court in the presence of Pilate.

After they listen to a couple of crucial witness, the Jewish Rabbis are in favour of liberation of Issa. They ritually clean their hands in front of Pilate, determined to pronounce the death penalty.

Here we clearly have a narrative that runs counter to the perspective given in the Synoptic Gospels.

Issa is sentenced to crucifixion, with two thieves:

«All day long the bodies of Issa and the two robbers hung upon the crosses, bleeding, guarded by the soldiers. The people stood all around and the relatives of the executed prayed and wept. When the sun went down, Issa's tortures ended. He lost consciousness and his soul disengaged itself from the body, to reunite with God. Thus ended the terrestrial existence of the reflection of the eternal Spirit under the form of a man who had saved hardened sinners and comforted the afflicted. Meanwhile, Pilate was afraid for what he had done, and ordered the body of the Saint to be given to his relatives, who put it in a tomb near to the place of execution. Great numbers of persons came to visit the tomb, and the air was filled with their wailings and lamentations. Three days later, the governor sent his soldiers to remove Issa's body and bury it in some other place, for he feared a rebellion among the people. The next day, when the people came to the tomb, they found it open and empty, the body of Issa being gone. Thereupon, the rumor spread that the Supreme Judge had sent His angels from Heaven, to remove the mortal remains of the saint in whom part of the divine Spirit had lived on earth.

When Pilate learned of this rumor, he grew angry and prohibited, under penalty of death, the naming of Issa, or praying for him to the Lord. But the people, nevertheless, continued to weep over Issa's death and to glorify their master; wherefore, many were carried into captivity, subjected to torture and put to death. And the disciples of Saint Issa departed from the land of Israel and went in all directions, to the heathen, preaching that they should abandon their gross errors, think of the salvation of their souls and earn the perfect bliss which awaits human beings in the immaterial world, full of glory, where the great Creator abides in all his immaculate and perfect majesty.

The heathen, their kings, and their warriors, listened to the preachers, abandoned their erroneous beliefs and forsook their priests and their idols, to celebrate the praises of the most wise Creator of the Universe, the King of Kings, whose heart is filled with infinite mercy»[43].

In the Appendix of his text, Notovitch writes the manuscripts he had the chance to translate reported more contents, beside *The unknown life of Jesus* and he made an effort to chronologically put in order the fragments of Issa's story.

However, the most important issue is that, after the publication of *La vie inconnue de Jesus Christ* — in 1894 — and

---

[43]*Ivi*, pp. 102-103.

the public accusation of fraud by the most important orientalist of that time — Max Müller — another person is reported to have analysed and translated the same manuscripts found by Notovitch.

We are alluding to Swami Abhedananda (1866-1939): vice-president of *Ramakrishna Math and Mission* in Belur Math (Kolkata) between 1921 and 1924, after he has travelled around US — teaching Vedanta — between 1897 and 1921.

In 1922 Swami Abhedananda begins a key journey into Kashmir and Tibet, with the purpose of looking for the famous manuscripts about Issa. After his experience in the field an account was published — in Bengali in 1929 and in English in 1987 — as the book *Swami Abhedananda's journey to Kashmir and Tibet*.

In its Appendix there is a Bengali and an English version of *The life of Saint Issa, best of the sons of men*.

Abhedananda had at his disposal the manuscripts for some time and he translated part of them, supported by an interpreter.

The Swami essentially confirms the authenticity of Notovitch's discovery but he does not create the presuppositions to go on studying the texts deeper. If you were to compare the level of study of this text with those found near the Dead Sea and those at Nag Hammadi there is a large gap.

For example, Notovitch's manuscripts should have been scientifically dated to demonstrate they really went back to a period immediately after Jesus' death (even if they were just a copy from an original in Pali language).

Indeed, these manuscripts could be a forgery produced in more recent times for different purposes.

In other words, it is reasonable to affirm that, without a serious verification of that material, it is difficult not to

doubt the authenticity of the text, even given the great benevolence Swami Abhedananda gave the text himself.
The relationship Jesus had with India led Abhedananda to propose, in one of the volumes of his *Opera Omnia*, one particularly intriguing argument.
He writes:

«The life of Jesus Christ as described in the Synoptic Gospels — the immaculate conception of a virgin mother, the miraculous birth, the story of the slaughter of infants by Herod — and the chief events of his life, all these seem like repetitions of what happened in the lives of Krishna (1400 B.C.) and of Buddha (547 B.C.). In fact, the idea of the incarnation of God is purely a Hindu idea. It was not known among the Jews. The Jews never accepted Christ as the incarnation of Divinity, but from the Vedic period the Hindus accepted many Avataras or incarnations of the Lord in human form, and this is at the foundation of the religion of the Hindus»[44].

Therefore I think it is reasonable — considering Jesus in an historical perspective — he could have achieved the idea of a man-God after he knew Hindu culture, being totally alien to religious perspectives of his own country.

However this hypothesis fails when looking at Jesus with a solid faith. If you considers him an incarnation of God, you can easily infer he did not need to go anywhere to be inspired, and was rather expressing an infused knowledge.

It is important to highlight again the differences between a faith's perspective and an historical one have to be constantly considered, representing a fundamental clue to proceed in exposing the topic of this book.

---

[44] *Complete works of Swami Abhedananda*, Ramakrishna Vedanta Math, Calcutta, 1967, Vol. II, p. 121.

After Abhedananda several people followed the traces of the *Unknown life of Jesus*. Nobody, according to what is commonly known, had access to the manuscripts today.

Nevertheless, as we have already mentioned and we will soon consider more in detail, Russian painter Nicholas Roerich, leading an expedition in several territories of India, Tibet, Sikkim, Chinese Turkestan and Mongolia (Altai) between 1923 and 1928, reports in his books *Heart of Asia* and *Altai and Himalaya* elements of a rich oral tradition about Issa.

In the next chapter we are going to consider another author who strongly supported the hypothesis of Indian years of Jesus, from a different point of view than the one of Notovitch, and the people who followed his path.

Mirzā Ghulām Ahmad and a heterodox Islamic eschatology

«O Muhammad, relate to them the story of Maryam in the Book (Al Qur'an) when she withdrew from her family to a place in the East. She chose to be secluded from them; then We sent to her Our angel and he appeared before her as a grown man.
She said: "I seek Rahman's (Allah's) protection against you, leave me alone if you are Godfearing".
He (The angel) said: "Don't be afraid. I am merely a messenger from your Rabb to tell you about the gift of a righteous son".
She said: "How shall I bear a son, when no man has ever touched me, nor am I unchaste?".
The angel replied: "So shall it be — your Rabb said: It is easy for Me. We wish to make him a Sign for mankind and a blessing from Us (Allah) — and this matter has already been decreed".
So she conceived the child and she retired with him to a remote place.
The pains of childbirth drove her to the trunk of a palm-tree. She cried in her anguish: "Ah! Would that I had died before this, and been long forgotten!".
An angel from beneath consoled her, saying: " Do not grieve! Your Rabb has provided a brook at your feet. If you shake the trunk of this palm-tree, it will drop fresh ripe dates upon you. So eat, drink and refresh yourself. If you see any human being, say: "I have vowed a fast for Rahman (Allah), so I will not speak to any human being today".

Carrying the baby, she came back to her people. They said: "O Maryam! You have brought something hard to believe!" — "O sister (a woman from the noble family) of Haroon! Your father was not a bad man nor your mother an unchaste woman!".
In response she merely pointed to the baby. They said: "How can we talk to a babe in the cradle?".

Whereupon the baby spoke out: "I'm indeed a servant of Allah, He has given me the Book and made me a Prophet. And He has made me blessed wherever I may be. He has commanded me to establish Salah (prayer) and give Zakat (obligatory charity), as long as I live. He has exhorted me to honor my mother and has not made me arrogant, disobedient. Peace be upon me the day I was born, the day I shall die and the Day I shall be raised to life again!".

Such was 'Isa (Jesus), the son of Maryam, and this is the true statement about him concerning which they are in doubt.

It is not befitting to the Majesty of Allah that He should beget a son! He is far above this; for when He decrees a matter He need only say: "Be!" and it is.

'Isa (Jesus) declared: "Verily Allah is my Rabb: therefore, serve Him (Alone). This is the Right Way"».

(*Al Qur'an*, XIX, 16-36)

Mirzā Ghulām Ahmad was born in 1835 in Qadian (a small town having, nowadays, around 40000 inhabitants, mostly Muslims), in the Punjab (India), in an aristocratic, Muslim, family.

As he grew he started to live almost in seclusion, studying several religious books and praying in the mosques.

He became progressively more active in the defence of Islam, authoritatively debating with members of other religions, mostly belonging to the Hindu reformist movement the *Arya Samaj* and with Christian missionaries.

In 1889 he claimed to have received a Divine revelation[45] legitimising him to take an oath of allegiance from some Muslim people who were already following him.

---

[45] The content of this revelation is reported on *www.alislam.org*:
«When thou hast determined, put thine trust in Allah. And build the Ark under Our eyes, as commanded by our revelation. Verily, those who swear allegiance to thee indeed swear allegiance to Allah. The hand of Allah is over their hand».

These are the humble beginnings of the *Ahmadiyya Muslim Community* (for further information about the Community please see the Appendix), whose founder claimed to be a *Mahdi* (a promised saviour).

He also claimed to be the Messiah, expected in several religious traditions, including, of course, the Islamic one.

It is also worth mentioning in Islamic eschatology it is predicted the *Mahdi*'s appearance, at the end of times, is to neutralise the *Dajjāl*: the "Antichrist".

After the appearance of the *Mahdi* or at the same time, according to other traditions, Jesus will return (in Arabic Isa o Issa, whose role in Islam is greatly more important than the average Christian can imagine) who, gathering all virtuous people, will kill the *Dajjāl* becoming the earthly king for forty years of perfect peace under Islamic rule.

In general, the Qur'an presents Jesus as a great prophet of God (*rasūl Allāh*) of human, not divine, nature but born by a virgin and a protagonist of several miracles «with Allah's permission».

It is important to repeat that a crucial belief about Jesus within Islamic tradition, is that he did not die on the cross («They say: "We have killed the Messiah, Isa, son of Maryam, the Rasool of Allah". Whereas in fact, neither did they kill him nor did they crucify him but they thought they did because the matter was made dubious for them»; *Al Qur'an*; IV,157) but he had a different destiny («The fact is that Allah took him up to Himself»; *Al Qur'an;* IV,158)[46], ready, in this way, to come back on the earth.

---

[46] I quote the Ahmadiyya version of the same Quranic verses:

«And their saying, 'We did kill the Messiah, Jesus, son of Mary, the Messenger of Allah;' whereas they slew him not, nor crucified him, but he was made to appear to them like one crucified; and those who differ therein are certainly in a state of doubt about it; they have no definite

Finally, Jesus will die of natural death (no man, in Islam, is immortal, even Muhammad died in 632), will be buried in Medina to revive in the apocalyptic *Yawm al-dīn* for the ultimate divine judgment when Allah will damn or save the dead of all human generations.

Worthy people will enjoy the pleasures of *Janna* (Heaven) while the damned ones will suffer in *Jahannam* (Islamic hell).

Mirzā Ghulām Ahmad, however, has promoted (as it has been already partially explained earlier in this book) an heterodox perspective where Jesus, despite suffering on the cross, did not die in that circumstance.

Taken down from the cross in apparent death or in coma, he was been transferred to the sepulchre by Nicodemus and Joseph of Arimathea and — treated with the afore mentioned *Marham-i-Isa* (Jesus' ointment) — he recovered quite quickly.

Up to this point in the narrative the view of Mirzā Ghulām Ahmad is not different from the one of *The Crucifixion, By An Eye-Witness*. It starts, however, to differ when Jesus, after he met his pupils, leaves Palestine to travel to India, with the purpose to preach to the dispersed tribes of Israel, mostly settled — in this perspective — between Afghanistan and Kashmir.

On the way to India, writes Mirzā Ghulām Ahmad, he crossed territories of modern day Syria, Iran, Afghanistan and Pakistan and, at an old age (approximately 120 years), he died from natural causes and he is buried in a sanctuary known, today, as the *Rozabal*, in the old town of Srinagar.

The supposed natural death of Jesus represents a crucial event in the perspective of Mirzā Ghulām Ahmad.

---

knowledge thereof, but only follow a conjecture; and they did not convert this conjecture into a certainty; On the contrary, Allah exalted him to Himself. And Allah is Mighty, Wise».

Indeed, considering again orthodox Islamic eschatology, Jesus will come back as Messiah, at the end of times, because he never died and «Allah took him up to Himself».

However, some concepts, wrote Mirzā Ghulām Ahmad, must be considered as metaphors.

The new Messiah, in his perspective, should not be somebody who already came but rather somebody else with his same nature, whose mission is to affirm the same principles.

Mirzā Ghulām Ahmad, as it had been anticipated, claimed to have received the revelation to be himself the chosen one for this task, even coherently with old prophecies, inaugurating a messianic era where the reasons of Islam can be affirmed through knowledge, persuasion, love for other people (despite the different creeds) and refusing, in the strongest way, any kind of violence.

We are going to consider, now, some crucial passages of his posthumous book (published in 1908) *Jesus in India*.

«I shall try to prove in this book», writes Mirzā Ghulām Ahmad in the introduction, «that Jesus did not die on the cross, nor did he go up to the heavens; nor should it be supposed that he would ever again come down to the earth. On the contrary, the fact of the matter is that he died at the age of one hundred and twenty years at Srinagar, Kashmir, where his tomb is still to be found in the Khan Yar quarter»[47].

To be successful in his difficult task, the founder of *Ahmadiyya Muslim Community* presents the eight chapters composing his *Jesus in India* where he arguments his thesis. Precisely:

1) Testimonies from the Gospels;

---

[47]Hadhrat Mirzā Ghulām Ahmad of Qadian, *Jesus in India*, Qadian, 2003, p. 14.

2) Testimonies from the Holy Quran and *Ahadith*;
3) Testimonies from medical literature;
4) Testimonies from historical records;
5) Testimonies from oral traditions which have been handed down from generation to generation;
6) Testimonies from miscellaneous circumstantial evidence;
7) Testimonies from logical argument;
8) Testimonies from divine revelation.

In the first chapter he quotes *Matthew's Gospel* (12 – 40):

«For as Jonah was three days and three nights in the whale's belly; so shall the son of man be three days and three nights in the heart of the earth».

It is evident, writes Mirzā Ghulām Ahmad, that Jonah arrived alive and he has remained alive in the whale's belly and, then, if Jesus was dead in the sepulchre upon his arrival, before later emerging alive then the similarity would have been neutralised.

«The truth», writes Mirzā Ghulām Ahmad, «is that Jesus was a true prophet of Allah» knowing he would have been saved from an accursed death.

It is worth recalling that, in the Muslim environment, it is highlighted crucifixion was the most infamous among death sentences and that the Sanhedrin insisted Jesus to be convicted to crucifixion to draggle his image in the centuries to come, trying to permanently erase him from the pages of history.

Nevertheless, a Prophet of Allah — in Muslim perspective — cannot endure that kind of affront and, for this reason, it is sure he didn't die on the cross.

Now, considering again specific point of view of Mirzā Ghulām Ahmad, if it is true Jesus didn't die on the cross (and here it is not different from the one of mainstream Islam), he has experienced, as it has already been mentioned, the ordeal of crucifixion to which, as a Prophet, he survived.

Coherently, even in the heterodox perspective of Mirzā Ghulām Ahmad, when the body was removed from the cross, it could only be alive (even if into a swoon or a coma), despite looking dead and, "after three days in the earth's belly" (as Jonah in whale's belly), he came back among men, simply alive because, till that moment, he had not experienced death.

It is worthy to mention that after Jesus' body was taken in custody by Joseph of Arimathea and Nicodemus, he was treated with *Marham-i-Isa* and, then, after a period probably longer than three days reported in the Gospels, he went to Galilee[48].

There he met his eleven disciples to whom he showed the fresh wounds. He ate some fish and some honey and, then, he slept with them.

Why would a resurrected man have eaten and slept? Asks Mirzā Ghulām Ahmad in his book.

Furthermore, resurrected bodies should be undamaged, not injured and disfigured.

Then, without going too far from what it is written in the Gospels, Mirzā Ghulām Ahmad claims Jesus went to Galilee after he survived the crucifixion, rather than after a resurrection.

After all, writes Mirzā Ghulām Ahmad, the execution itself was suspicious (on this point, as we've already written, there are several perplexities).

---

[48]It is right to underline that Jesus' transfer to Galilee has been prophesied by him in Matthew 26, 32: «But after I have been raised, I will go before you to Galilee».

The torture of crucifixion was designed to make the convicts suffer for some days, without food and water, under the merciless sun.

In case of doubts about death, the convicts would have their legs broken (generally at knee height) «and so deprived of any strength whatsoever to maintain the weight of the body. The body would drop, and death by asphyxiation rapidly followed»[49].

From the Gospels we know that it is what has happened to two thieves crucified at left and right side of Jesus.

Instead he has been spared. Longinus' spear has been pierced through his ribs from where poured blood and water (and this, as we have already argued, could be a proof that blood circulation was still active and, then, the body still alive) and he has been lowered from the cross after just few hours of torture.

Indeed his crucifixion has taken place on Friday.

The day after was *Sabbath* and it was also a Jew festivity: *Fasah*.

According to Judaic law, writes Mirzā Ghulām Ahmad, it was rigorously forbidden the convicts remained on the cross on *Sabbath* or even the night before.

Jews followed lunar calendar and, then, each day was computed at the beginning of sunset of former one (then *Sabbath* at sunset of Friday).

Therefore, the convicts were crucified on Friday to be lowered from the cross before sunset of the same day.

It is reasonable to infer there was not enough time to die. Indeed, to quicken the execution, respecting the prescriptions of Judaic law, the legs of two thieves have been broken.

---

[49] Michael Baigent, *The Jesus' papers*, Harper, San Francisco, 2006, p. 127

Then, Jesus' body was given to Joseph of Arimathea, his supporter or, maybe, his disciple and the owner of sepulchre where he was carried.

Mirzā Ghulām Ahmad — as well as other scholars — supported the thesis Pilate himself, even listening to his wife's advise[50], had a crucial role to save Jesus' life and it was even for this reason everything was organized to crucify him on Friday and then to give the body to Joseph of Arimathea who, before sunset, warmly claimed execution was completed and the body was dead. Till now there is a full convergence between the thesis of Mirzā Ghulām Ahmad and the one proposed in *The Crucifixion, By An Eye-Witness*.

We consider now the second chapter of *Jesus in India*, where Mirzā Ghulām Ahmad quotes the verse 157 of *Sura* 4 of Quran. It is important to clarify this Sura has been translated, from Arabic, in slightly — but crucially — different manners.

I quote below the version proposed in *Al Qur'an* published by *The Institute of Islamic Knowledge* and, then, the one proposed by *Ahmadiyya Muslim Community*, published by *Islam International Publications Limited* (they are both mentioned in the bibliography):

«They say: "We have killed the Messiah, Isa, son of Maryam, the Rasool of Allah". Whereas in fact, neither did they kill him nor did they crucify him but they thought they did because the matter was made dubious for them. Those who differ therein are in doubt. They have no real knowledge, they follow nothing but mere conjecture, certainly, they did not kill him».

---

[50]«While he was sitting on the judgment seat, his wife sent to him, saying, "Have nothing to do with that just Man, for I have suffered many things today in a dream because of Him». (Matthew, 27/19)

«And for their saying, "We did slay the Messiah Jesus, son of Maryam (Mary), the Messenger of Allah", whereas they slew him not, nor did they bring about his death on the cross, but he was made to appear to them like one crucified; and those who differ therein are certainly in a state of doubt about it. They have no certain knowledge thereof, they only pursue a conjecture; and they did not arrive at a certainty concerning it».

This verse, in the opinion of Mirzā Ghulām Ahmad, can be easily interpreted as a confirm of hypothesis Jesus, despite suffering the ordeal of crucifixion, did not die on the cross.

The leading characters of the quoted *Sura* — the Jews — have never been able to demonstrate, writes Mirzā Ghulām Ahmad, how Jesus could die after just three hours or a little more on the cross, without having the bones of his legs broken.

He even quotes verse 46 of the third *Sura*, where it is reported an Annunciation to Mary, claiming the 'other world' that is written about could be the land of the Punjab from where Jesus could enter India, after ordeal of crucifixion:

«When the angels said: "O Maryam, Allah gives you thee good news with a Word from Him that you will be given a son: his name will be Al Maseeh (Messiah), Isa (Jesus Christ), the son of Maryam. He will be notable in this world and the hereafter; and will be from those who are very close to Allah"».

On his way to India, mostly in Afghanistan and Kashmir, he found members of the ten, lost tribes of Israel (we will consider this issue more in detail in the next paragraph).

To confirm this, Mirzā Ghulām Ahmad reveals the discovery, in Punjab, of a coin with the name of Jesus written in the Pali language. It is a proof, he claims, Jesus has been welcomed and highly honoured in the Punjab by a King, who became his pupil.

In the recent documentary, by the Film Division of the Government of India, *The Rozabal shrine of Srinagar* a coin representing Yuzu Asaph is shown.

Finally, in the second chapter of his book, Mirzā Ghulām Ahmad quotes one collection of *Ahadith*[51] known as *Kanz-ul-Ummal*, in particular what it is written in its second volume by Abu Huraira[52]:

«God revealed to Jesus thus: "O Jesus keep on moving from one place to another", go from one country to another lest thou should recognised and persecuted»[53].
[...]
«Jesus continuously travelled from one country to another, wherever he happened to be at nightfall, he would partake of the vegetables of the jungle and drink fresh water»[54].
[...]
«The Holy Prophet said: "The people most favoured in the sight of God are the Ghareeb". When asked what was meant by the

---

[51] «Hadīth, Arabic Ḥadīth ("News" or "Story"), also spelled Hadīt, record of the traditions or sayings of the Prophet Muhammad, revered and received as a major source of religious law and moral guidance, second only to the authority of the Qur'ān, the holy book of Islam. It might be defined as the biography of Muhammad perpetuated by the long memory of his community for their exemplification and obedience. The development of Hadith is a vital element during the first three centuries of Islamic history, and its study provides a broad index to the mind and ethos of Islam».

www.britannica.com/topic/Hadith

[52] I've already shortly presented Abu Huraira in the footnote number 9.

[53] HadhratMirzāGhulāmAhmadofQadian, *Jesus in India*, Qadian, 2003, p. 63.

[54] *Ibidem.*

term Ghareeb, he replied "They are the people who, like Jesus, the Messiah, have to flee from their country to save their faith"»[55].

Considering now the chapter of Mirzā Ghulām Ahmad's book (available on line the website of Ahmadiyya Muslim Jama'at *alislam.org*) about medical literature, he focuses his attention on the ointment of Jesus we have already mentioned: the *Marham-i-Isa*.

He lists several medical books (thirty three) where it is mentioned.

The most important one, as we told, is *Canon of Avicenna* which, along with many other texts listed, has been crucial for training several European, Arab, Persian doctors in a remarkable period.

According to the *Canon of Avicenna*, the ointment of Jesus contains twelve ingredients, as the number of apostles.

Jesus' possible itinerary to India

Though, one of the most interesting issues considered in *Jesus in India*, is the itinerary of Jesus, from Palestine to India, after the ordeal of crucifixion.

It is corroborated by some historical sources.

Mirzā Ghulām Ahmad quotes *Rauzat-us-Safaa*[56], an historical text in Persian language:

«Jesus was named the Messiah because he was a great traveller. [...]

---

[55] *Ibidem*.
[56] In English *Garden of Purity concerning the biography of the Prophets and Kings and Caliphs*. It is a Persian historical book, in seven volumes, authored, by Mohammad ibn Khwāndshāh ibn Mahmud (1433-1498).

He used to wander from country to country and city to city. He slept wherever the night found him. He ate vegetables of the jungle, drank fresh water and travelled on foot.
[...]
Journeying from his country, he arrived at Nasibain, which lay at a distance of several hundred koses from his home. He was accompanied by a few of his disciples whom he sent into the city to preach. In the city, however, false and unfounded rumours were current about Jesus and his mother. The governor of the city, therefore, arrested the disciples and summoned Jesus.
Jesus miraculously healed some patients and showed some other miracles. As a result, the king of the territory of Nasibain, with all his armies and his people, became his follower»[57].

According to what we read, Nasibain could be the first stop of Jesus' travel to the East.

Actually, I had the privilege to consult directly one version in English of *Rauzat-us-Safaa* in Patna's *Khuda Bakhsh Oriental Public Library* and I've verified Jesus' stay in Nasibain is not connected, in any way, to his hypothetical journey after the crucifixion, because the book in analysis is adherent to the mainstream Islamic escathological perspective.

However, thinking freely, it is bizarre what it is mentioned in *Rauzat-us-Safaa* (whose chapter about Jesus' stay in Nasibain has been fully included in the Appendix), a prestigious historical book, is totally missing in the New Testament and in apocryphal Gospels.

The place itself, Nasibain, is quite unusual and relatively distant from historical ones related with Jesus.

Then it is reasonable that the chronicle of Jesus' stay in an area located, today, between Turkey and Syria could be related with a period of his life — following the ordeal of crucifixion — where he lived far from his native place.

---

[57] Hadhrat Mirzā Ghulām Ahmad of Qadian, *Jesus in India*, pp. 78-79.

It is even reasonable this period of his life remained in the shadows within the traditional Christian culture.

After his stay in Nasibain, according to the book of Mirzā Ghulām Ahmad, Jesus journeyed on, through Persia, into the area known today as Afghanistan, where some of the ten, Lost Tribes of Israel had settled.

Regarding the possible Jewish origin of the Afghan people (a hypothesis strongly supported by Mirzā Ghulām Ahmad, who claimed the word itself *Afghan* has a Jew origin, meaning *brave*) scholars have been debating it for a long time.

In the beautiful library of Patna *Bihar Research Society* I was able to consult the book *A History of Afghanistan*, by Sir Percy Sykes, where it is reported:

«A protest must here be made against the erroneous view that the Afghans are members of the lost tribes of Israel, which various writers, including Bellew and Holdich, advocated actually this theory is of purely literary origin and is merely an example of the widespread custom among Moslems of claiming descent from some personage mentioned in the Koran or other sacred work. In the case of the Afghans, they claim Malik Talut or King Saul as their ancestor»[58].

However, the hypothesis of the Jew origin of Afghan people, according to Sir Percy Sykes, is not confined to Mirzā Ghulām Ahmad and other scholars, we will see, have followed this same trail.

Certainly the issue of the Lost Tribes of Israel has a crucial part to play in the search for the Indian years of Jesus, mostly during his "second life", after the ordeal of crucifixion because, according to the *Gospel of Matthew* (15, 24),

---

[58] Sir Percy Sykes, *A history of Afghanistan*, Vol. I, Macmillan & Co, London, 1940, p. 13.

his fundamental mission was to preach to their members: «I was not sent except to the lost sheep of the house of Israel».

Indeed a Jewish presence in Afghanistan, in some areas of modern day Pakistan and, overall, in Kashmir would have, surely, represented a crucial motivation, for Jesus, to visit those lands.

In the Appendix of his book, Mirzā Ghulām Ahmad quotes several sources corroborating his hypothesis starting from a — frankly very generic — affirmation by Flavius Josephus, famous author of *The Jewish War* and *Jewish Antiquities*:

«The *ten tribes are beyond Euphrates* till now, and are an immense multitude».

Still focused on Afghanistan, Mirzā Ghulām Ahmad quotes, directly, H.W. Bellew who, in 1880, wrote in his *The races of Afghanistan*:

«The traditions of this people refer them to Syria as the country of their residence at the time they were carried away into captivity by Bukhtunasar (Nebuchadnezzar), and planted as colonists in different parts of Persia and Media. From these positions they, at some subsequent period, emigrated eastward into the mountainous country of Ghor, where they were called by the neighbouring peoples "Bani Afghan" and "Bani Israil", or children of Afghan and children of Israel.
[…]
It is stated in the *Tabacati Nasiri* — a historical work which contains, among other information, a detailed account of the conquest of the country by Changhiz Khan — that in the time of the native Shansabi dynasty there was a people called Bani Israil living in that country, and that some of them were extensively engaged in trade with the countries around»[59].

---

[59] In: Mirzā Ghulām Ahmad, *Jesus in India*, op. cit., p. 132.

The library of Mirzā Ghulām Ahmad family was perhaps the richest within hundreds of kilometres.

It did not lack Encyclopaedias.

The author of *Jesus in India* quotes a couple of them, again in the Appendix of his book.

Cyclopedia of India and of Eastern and Southern Asia (Bernard Quaritch, London, 1885), about *Afghanistan* reports:

«Pukhtun is the national appellation of the Afghans proper; but the Afghans and Pathans also designate themselves Ban-i-Israel, and some claim direct descent from Saul, king of Israel»[60].

While *Cyclopedia of India of Geography* (Richard Griffin and Co. London and Glasgow, 1856) reports:

«The name Afghan is not used by the people themselves, they call themselves Pooshton and in the plural Pooshtauneh, from which, perhaps, comes the name Putan or Patan, given to them in India. They trace their origin to Saul, King of Israel, calling themselves Ben-i-Israel. According to Sir A. Burnes, their tradition is that they were transplanted by the King of Babylon from the Holy Land to Ghore, lying to the N.W. of Cabool and lived as jews till A.D. 682, when they were converted to Mahometanism by an Arab chief, Khaled-ibn-Abdalla, who had married a daughter of an Afghan chief. No historical evidence has ever been adducted in support of this origin and it is perhaps a mere invention, founded upon the facts mentioned in 2 Kings XVIII, 11. However this may be, all travelers agree that the people differ strikingly from the neighbouring nations and have, among themselves, one common origin. They are said, by some, to resemble Jews very much in form and feature; and they are divided into several tribes, inhabiting separate territories and remaining almost unmixed»[61].

---

[60] *Ivi.*, p. 134.
[61] *Ivi*, pp. 140-141.

Finally I think it is interesting to mention, among supporters of the Jewish origin of Afghans, Sir William Jones, founder of *Royal Asiatic Society of Bengal* in 1784 (then inherited from India with simplified name of *Asiatic Society,* prestigious centre of studies e researches in the heart of Kolkata) who strongly contributed to the birth of modern Indology.

We will consider again, in this book, the issue of *Bani Israel* — children of Israel — according to more recent studies.

Continuing to probe the book *Jesus in India*, it cannot be excluded, writes Mirzā Ghulām Ahmad, Jesus spent a period in Afghanistan where, maybe, he even had a wife.

One of the Afghan tribe is known as Isa Khel and it could include descendants of Jesus.

This thesis can be corroborated by O.M. Burke book — far more recently then Mirzā Ghulām Ahmad's book — *Among the dervishes*, written after a long experience in the field.

One chapter of this book is titled: *The Followers of Jesus.*

Quoting it:

«The followers of Isa, son of Maryam — Jesus the son of Mary — generally call themselves Moslems and inhabit a number of villages scattered throughout the Western area of Afghanistan whose centre is Herat. I had heard of them several times but considered that they were probably people who had been converted by European missionaries from Eastern Persia, or else that they were a relic of the times when Herat had been a flourish bishopric of the Nestorian rite, before the Arabs conquered Persia in the seventh and eighth centuries. But, from their own accounts and what I could observe, they seem to come from some much older source. I found them through one of the deputies of the Mir of Gazarga, the descendant of Mohammed under whose protection they are. Gazarga is the shrine where Abdullah Ansar, a Sufi mystic and great local saint, is buried in a magnificent tomb formerly much visited by the emperors of India and other notables.

There must be about a thousand of these Christians. Their chief is Abba Yahiyya (Father John), who can recite the succession of teachers through nearly sixty generations to Isa, son of Mary, of "Nazara", the Kashmiri.
According to these people, Jesus escaped from the Cross, was hidden by friends, was helped to flee to India, where he had been before during his youth, and settled in Kashmir, where he is revered as an ancient teacher, Yuz Asaf. It is from this period of the supposed life of Jesus that these people claim to have got their message»[62].

I think this is a significant testimony, independent from the Punjabi or Kashmiri accounts, fully confirming the thesis of the Indian years of Jesus.

It is a second piece of the puzzle outlining the possible itinerary followed by Jesus after the crucifixion and it sheds light on the period he would have spent in Nasibain.

The third piece of the puzzle is located in Pakistan, where there exists a purported tomb of Mary (the mother of Jesus) but we will consider this issue, in detail, later.

At the moment, we remain in Afghanistan, with the Followers of Jesus and Mr. Burke.

Quoting from his book:

«I had several conversations with the Abba. [...][He] lived on a farm, and like all the "Christians" says that their teacher stipulated that his followers should always have a worldly vocation. Jesus, according to this community, was a carpenter and also a shepherd. He had the power to perform miracles, and he did indeed "die for the sake of his people". This death, astonishingly enough, is not the death generally assumed. The death was a real one, but it took place long before Jesus started his mission, and it was as a result of this experience that he met God and was sent back to mankind

---

[62]Burke O.M., *Among the dervishes*, The Octagon Press, London, 1993, p. 111.

to warn them of their possible fate if they did not seek love and truth.

The "Traditions of the Masih" (anointed one) is the holy book of the community. They do not believe in the New Testament; or, rather, they say that these Traditions are the New Testament, and that the Gospels which we have are partly true but generally written by people who did not understand the teaching of the Master.

Abba Yahiyya, a towering figure with the face of a saint, was certainly an erudite man, and he knew his own scriptures, plus a great deal of the Jewish writings, very well indeed. He had heard of the teachings of the "heretics" as he called what we would call the various sects of Christians known to us; and he wanted no part of them.

"My son", he said, in his softly accented Persian, "these people are reading and repeating a part of the story. They have completely misunderstood the message. We have the story told us by the Master, and through Him we will be saved and made whole. Some of the events in that document which you call the Bible are true, but a great deal is made up or imagined or put in for less than worthy reasons. Isa lived for over thirty years after the materials you have were completed, and he told us what was true".

Briefly, the doctrine is that Jesus was the Son of God because He had attained that rank through his goodness and sacrifices. Thus He was equal to a divine person. He came after John the Baptist, who himself had reached the highest degree of development possible at that time. John baptized with water, Jesus with spirit and fire. These were the three stages of understanding, which were taught by our Christians.

There was a great deal of confusion at first, because I was talking about sacraments and being saved, while it took me some time to realize that Abba John's people regarded baptism, the Holy Ghost and the Kingdom of God to be three stages in a system of human illumination. This is what they claim is the function of the Church: the preservation of and administration of these three "developments" for the worshippers.

There is a ritual meal, like the Last Supper, but this is carried out once a week. Bread and wine are eaten, but as symbolic of the grosser and finer nutritions which are the experiences of attainment of nearness to God.

While it is possible to consider these people as mere heretics, or else as followers of someone else who impersonated Jesus, yet I was singularly impressed by their piety, their feeling of certainty, their simplicity and lack of unpleasant forms of fervor which often finds in minority cults. They were convinced, too, that the day would come when the world would discover the truth about Jesus. When this took place, it would be the mission of the Followers to come out into the open and teach those who wanted to believe in Jesus the methods by which a man or a woman could "enter the Kingdom"»[63].

Was Jesus the expected Buddha Maitreya?

Approaching the conclusion of Mirzā Ghulām Ahmad's book, he analyses some similarities between Buddha and Jesus, for instance common honorary titles, biographical events (as to have been both tempted by the devil) and doctrinal contents.

Mirzā Ghulām Ahmad claimed Jesus' doctrine was predicted in Buddhist texts and Buddha himself had clearly prophesied the Palestinian master would have been his successor, with a wider number of followers.

In other words: Jesus was the expected Buddha Maitreya[64]. Indeed, wrote Mirzā Ghulām Ahmad, the Pali[65] equivalent of Maitreya is Metteya. It is well known, the author wrote in his

---

[63]*Ivi*, pp. 112-113.
[64]"Buddha of the future" in Buddhist escathology.
[65]Pali is a dialect of Sanskrit, holy language of Theravada Buddhism, used to write first Buddhist holy books, united in *Tipitaka* (Three baskets) and usually qualified as "Pali Canon".

treatise *Jesus in India*, when one word shifts from one language to another one, undergoes some phonetic changes.

The famous orientalist Max Müller wrote in the eleventh volume of his monumental work *Sacred books of the east* that, for instance, *th* of English alphabet becomes *s* in Persian and Arabic.

Because of that, the Hebrew word Mashiha (Messiah) could be the Semitic equivalent of Metteya.

In this perspective Jesus' coming on the earth would have been announced in *Cakkavatti Sīhanāda Suttanta*, within the *Pali Canon* where it is claimed:

«[...]there will arise in the world a Blessed Lord, an Arahant fully-enlightened Buddha named Metteyya, endowed with wisdom and conduct, a Well-Farer, Knower of the worlds, incomparable Trainer of men to be tamed, Teacher of gods and humans, enlightened and blessed, just as I am now. He will thoroughly know by his own super-knowledge, and proclaim, this universe with its devas and maras and Brahmas, its ascetics and Brahmins, and this generation with its princes and people, just as I do now. He will teach the Dhamma, lovely in its beginning, lovely in its middle, lovely in its ending, in the spirit and in the letter, and proclaim, just as I do now, the holy life in its fullness and purity. He will be attended by a company of thousands of monks, just as I am attended by a company of hundreds».

The problem of many prophecies (and this one is no exception to this role) is the difficulty in understanding when they will become true.

Perhaps the most fitting example, in this regard, is the "delay of *Parousia*", "the return of Christ on the earth to join his devotees at the end of the history". A delay that is still prolonging today.

In the case of the Sublime Metteya, however, Mirzā Ghulām Ahmad proposes an *escamotage*, that is another prophecy according to which the doctrine taught by the Buddha would have remained intact for only five hundred years.

I have found it in the brilliant book of Ananda Coomaraswamy *Buddha and the Gospel of Buddhism*.

Actually it is not easy to find the passage I am going to quote because it is unflattering towards women.

We can go back to the time of the Buddha and women have just been admitted in the *Sangha* (community of pupil of Gautama Siddharta at the origin of later monastic orders).

According to Coomaraswamy — and also to German historian of Buddhism Hermann Oldenberg who highlight what it could, today, be considered a tendential misogyny present in the Buddhist field, mostly at the beginning — Buddha accepted the women in the *Sangha* more for kindness than for being convinced it was the right thing to do.

Then he says to his favourite disciple:

«If, Ananda, women had not retired from household life to the houseless one, under the doctrine and discipline announced by the Tathagata, religion, Ananda, would long endure; a thousand years would the good doctrine abide. But since, Ananda, women have now retired from the household life to the houseless one, under the doctrine and discipline announced by the Tathagata, not long, Ananda, will religion endure; but five hundred years, Ananda, will the good doctrine abide»[66].

We know well between Buddha and Jesus there is a five hundred years gap.

Considering the two prophecies together, Mirzā Ghulām Ahmad proposes the thesis at the peak of the decadence of the "good doctrine" — five hundred years after the

---

[66] Ananda Coomaraswamy, *Buddha and the Gospel of Buddhism*, G.P. Putnam's Sons, New York, 1916, p. 162.

teachings of Buddha — once the Buddhist monastic community was well settled, "the following Buddha", "named Metteya", would have arrived "Teacher of gods and humans, enlightened and blessed".

Born in a land other than India, his name would have been slightly modified and, instead of Metteya, he would have been known as "the Messiah". According to this theory we are talking exactly about Jesus, later considered, in *Vajrayana* Buddhism, as a *Bodhisattva*.

In general, I think it is quite reasonable to affirm that far from being two watertight compartments, Buddhism and Christianity — even regardless of specific prophecies — can be considered as more or less deeply connected from a common thread and I think extensive research should be done in this field.

Mirzā Ghulām Ahmad, at the end of nineteenth century — regardless of whether his conclusions are shared — did his own.

The esoteric approach; visits of Akashic records

Leaving the heterodox perspective of Mirzā Ghulām Ahmad we are now going to consider another very different area relating to the possible Indian years of Jesus.

The books we are going to mention have been written — in line with the first version, in Urdu, of *Jesus in India* — at the beginning of Twentieth century.

We are going to present briefly their contents while proceeding in chronological order.

We can begin by covering what Professor Erwin Laszlo[67] writes in his book *Science and the Akashic Field*.

«*Akasha* is a Sanskrit word meaning "ether": all-pervasive space. Originally signifying "radiation" or "brilliance", in Indian philosophy akasha was considered the first and most fundamental of the five elements — the others being vata (air), agni (fire), ap (water) and prithivi (earth). Akasha embraces the properties of all five elements: it is the womb from which everything we perceive

---

[67] Quoting from his website *ervinlaszlo.com*:

«*Iam Ervin Laszlo, Founder and President of The Club of Budapest, Director and Co-Founder of the Ervin Laszlo Institute for Advanced Study (ELIAS) and of the Laszlo New-Paradigm Leadership Center (Italy)*, Member of the *Hungarian Academy of Science*, Fellow of the *World Academy of Arts and Sciences*, Member of the *International Academy of Philosophy of Science*, Member of the *International Academy of Systems Research and Cybernetics*, Senator of the *International Medici Academy*, and Editor of the international periodical *World Futures: The Journal of General Evolution*. I am the author or co-author of fifty-four books translated into as many as twenty-three languages, and the editor of another thirty volumes including a four-volume encyclopedia».

with our senses has emerged and into which everything will ultimately redescend. "The Akashic Record" (also called "The Akashic Chronicle") is the enduring record of all that happens, and has ever happened, in the whole of the universe»[68].

In the following paragraphs we will present five "visitors" (through astral travels or in altered states of consciousness) to The Akashic Record.

Their visits have been covered in several books.

Levi H. Dowling

«Levi H. Dowling was born Friday morning, May 18, 1844, at Belleville, Ohio. His father, Scotch-Welsh descent, was a pioneer preacher among the Disciples of Christ. Levi was always a student of the deeper things of life. At the age of thirteen, in his first public debate, he took the negative side against a Presbyterian Elder on "The Everlasting Punishment of the Wicked".

He began preaching at the age of sixteen; and at the age of eighteen was pastor of a small church. He entered the United States Army at the age of twenty as Chaplain, and served in his capacity to the end of the Civil War. In 1866-7 he was a student at Northwestern Christian University at Indianapolis, Indiana. The next year he began publishing Sunday School Literature, issuing Sunday School Lesson Papers, Song Books and a Children's Sunday School Paper. Much of his time was devoted to the cause of Prohibition. He was a graduate of two medical colleges and practiced medicine for a number of years. He finally retired from the medical profession to resume literary work.

Early in his life, when but a mere lad, he had a vision in which he was told that he was to "build a white city". This vision was repeated three times with years intervening. The building of the "white city" was "The Aquarian Gospel of Jesus Christ". This

---

[68] Erwin Laszlo, *Science and the Akashic Field*, Inner Traditions, Rochester, Vermont (USA), 2007, p. 1.

book was transcribed between the early morning hours of two and six — the absolutely "quiet hours".
Levi passed from earth-life August 13, 1911»[69].

I have scrupulously read *The Aquarian Gospel* and I have found it a particularly fluent and intriguing text.

It is quite detailed but, of course, I cannot claim its religious authenticity.

Dowling describes, over the course of around sixty pages, Jesus' journeys during his "lost years".

Between the paragraphs sixth and eleven he writes on the topic of: "*Life and works of Jesus in India, in Tibet and Western India, in Persia, in Assyria, in Greece, in Egypt.*"

Dowling writes that, far from doing the carpenter's repetitive work in Palestine, Aquarian Jesus did not get bored at all!

According to what is written in *The Aquarian Gospel*, a royal prince of India, Ravanna of Orissa, notices Jesus while he was talking in Jewish temple, in Jerusalem, among the Rabbis.

Amazed by his speech and his wisdom, he decides to follow the young Jesus to Nazareth.

There he gave a feast for all the people of the town. Jesus and his family were the honoured guests.

Not long after this he asked Joseph to be the patron of the child Jesus, taking him to the East.

Not without sorrow, Joseph and Mary gave consent.

An important stage of Jesus' stay in India, according to *The Aquarian Gospel*, was the period of approximately four years he spent in Puri's *Jagannath Temple*, as in "Tibetan version" of the 'Life of St Issa' scroll, disclosed by Notovitch:

---

[69] Levi H. Dowling, *The Aquarian Gospel of Jesus Christ*, L.N. Fowler & CO. LTD, London, 1972, p. 3.

«Among the priests of Jagannath was one who loved the Jewish boy. Lamaaas Bramas was the name by which the priest was known.

One day as Jesus and Lamaas walked alone in plaza Jagannath, Lamaas said, My Jewish master, what is truth?

And Jesus said, Truth is the only thing that changes not.

In all the world there are two things; the one is truth; the other is falsehood; and truth is that which is, and falsehood that which seems to be. Now truth is aught and has no cause, and yet it is the cause of everything.

Falsehood is naught, and yet it is the manifest of aught.

Whatever has been made will be unmade; that which begins must end.

All things that can be seen by human eyes are manifests of aught, are naught, and so must pass away.

The things we see are but reflexes just appearing, while the ethers vibrate so and so, and when conditions change they disappear.

The Holy Breath is truth; is that which was, and is, and evermore shall be; it cannot change nor pass away.

Lamas said. You answer well; now, what is man?

And Jesus said, Man is the truth and falsehood strangely mixed. Man is the breath made flesh; so truth and falsehood are conjoined in him; and then they strive, and naught goes down and man as truth abides.

Again Lamaas asked, What do you say of power? And Jesus said, It is a manifest; is the result of force; it is but naught; it is illusion, nothing more. Force changes not, but power changes as the ethers change.

Force is the will of God and is omnipotent, and power is that will in manifest, directed bhy the Breath.

There is a power in the winds, a power in the waves, a power in the lightning's stroke, a power in the human arm, a power in the eye.

The ethers cause these powers to be, and thought of Elohim, of angel, man or other thinking thing, directs the force; when it has done its work the power is no more.

Again Lamaas asked, Of understanding what have you to say? And Jesus said, It is the rock on which man builds himself; it is the gnosis of the aught and of the naught, of falsehood and of truth. It is the knowledge of the lower self; the sensing of the powers of man himself.

Again Lamaas asked, Of wisdom what have you to say? And Jesus said, It is the consciousness that man is aught; that God and man are one; that naught is naught; that power is but illusion; that heaven and earth and hell are not above, around, below, but in; which in the light of aught becomes the naught, and God is all.

Lamaas asked, Pray, what is faith? And Jesus said, Faith is the surety of the omnipotence of God and man; the certainty that man will reach deific life. Salvation is a ladder reaching from the heart of man to heart of God. It has three steps; belief is first, and this is what man thinks, perhaps, is truth. Fruition is the last and this is man himself, the truth. Belief is lost in faith; and in fruition faith is lost; and man is saved when he has reached deific life; when he and God are one»[70].

In *The Aquarian Gospel*, as in the documents found by Notovitch in Ladakh, Jesus is a big supporters of equality of men, firmly opposing India's caste system.

In the following passage Jesus challenges the ideas they expose to him in *Jagannath Temple*, the caste dimension prescribing men and women must be divided by color (indeed, the original Sanskrit word designating castes, in India, is *varna*: color): white the Brahmins, produced by the mouth of Purusa (the mythical cosmic man), red the *kshatrya*, produced by his hand, yellow the *vaisya*, by his belly and black the *sudra*, by his foot[71].

---

[70] *Ivi*, pp. 57-58.
[71] «When they divided Purusa how many portions did they make? What do they call his mouth, his arms? What do they call his thighs and feet? The Brahman was his mouth, of both his arms was the Rajanya made. His thighs became the Vaisya, from his feet the Sudra was produced». (Rgveda, X,90-11,12)

«And Jesus said, Then Parabrahm is not a God of justice and of right; for with his own strong hand he has exalted one and brought another low. And Jesus said no more to them, but looking up to heaven he said, My Father-God, who was, and is, and evermore shall be; who holds within thy hands the scales of justice and of right; Who in the boundlessness of love has made all men to equal be. The white, the black, the yellow and the red can look up in thy face and say, Our Father-God. Thou Father of the human race, I praise thy name»[72].

According to this version of the life of Jesus, his declaration of equality of all men could have resulted in great harm for him. However, thanks to the mediation of his friend Lamaas, in the report of *The Aquarian Gospel*, Jesus was saved from the anger of the members of the high castes.

He "found a shelter with the black and yellow men, the servants and the tillers of the soil. To them he first made known the gospel of equality; he told them of the Brotherood of Man, the Fatherood of God"[73].

Rudolf Steiner

«Rudolf Steiner, (born February 27, 1861, Kraljević, Austria — died March 30, 1925, Dornach, Switzerland), Austrian-born spiritualist, lecturer, and founder of anthroposophy, a movement based on the notion that there is a spiritual world comprehensible to pure thought but accessible only to the highest faculties of mental knowledge.
Attracted in his youth to the works of Goethe, Steiner edited that poet's scientific works and from 1889 to 1896 worked on the standard edition of his complete works at Weimar. During this period he wrote his *Die Philosophie der Freiheit* (1894; "The Phi-

---

[72]*Ivi*, p. 60.
[73]*Ibidem*.

losophy of Freedom"), then moved to Berlin to edit the literary journal *Magazin für Literatur* and to lecture.

Coming gradually to believe in spiritual perception independent of the senses, he called the result of his research "anthroposophy," centring on "knowledge produced by the higher self in man".

In 1912 he founded the Anthroposophical Society.

Steiner believed that humans once participated more fully in spiritual processes of the world through a dreamlike consciousness but had since become restricted by their attachment to material things.

The renewed perception of spiritual things required training the human consciousness to rise above attention to matter.

The ability to achieve this goal by an exercise of the intellect is theoretically innate in everyone.

In 1913 at Dornach, near Basel, Switzerland, Steiner built his first Goetheanum, which he characterized as a "school of spiritual science." After a fire in 1922, it was replaced by another building.

The Waldorf School movement, derived from his experiments with the Goetheanum, by the early 21st century had more than 1000 schools around the world. Other projects that grew out of Steiner's work include communities for persons with disabilities; a therapeutic clinical centre at Arlesheim, Switzerland; scientific and mathematical research centres; and schools of drama, speech, painting, and sculpture. Among Steiner's varied writings are *The Philosophy of Spiritual Activity* (1894), *Occult Science: An Outline* (1913), and *Story of My Life* (1924)»[74].

Rudolf Steiner's book *The Fifth Gospel, Investigation of the Akasha Chronicle* has been composed from the content of seven conferences held in Oslo from first to sixth of October 1913 and in Cologne from the seventeenth to the eighteenth of December of the same year.

During his conferences, Steiner asserts from Christ it is derived a great action whose effects

---

[74] Quoted from: *www.britannica.com/biography/Rudolf-Steiner*.

to all those who have followed the great teacher are mostly independent from subsequent speculations, starting from the ones of Fathers of the Church and, then, of Scholasticism and even of Anthroposophy.

In other words, according to Steiner, the remarkable rise of Christianity and its deep transformation of the world were not the product of the intellect, but of a deeper awakening of Human souls (mostly among simple people) that Christ was able to inspire.

Quoting from the book *The Fifth Gospel, Investigation of the Akasha Chronicle* :

«The Christian impulses have spread by strange channels – in the absence, so it appears, of intellectuality, learning, erudition.
Christianity has spread irrespectively of the views of its adherents or opponents – even appearing in an inverted form in the domain of modern materialism. But what exactly is it that spreads? It is not the ideas nor is it the science of Christianity; nor can we say that it is the morality instilled by Christianity. Think only of the moral life of men in those times and we shall find much justification for the fury levelled by men who represented Christianity against those who were its real or alleged enemies.
Even the moral power that might have been possessed by souls without much intellectual education will not greatly impress us. What, then, is this mysterious impulse which makes its victorious way through the world? Let us turn here to Spiritual Science, to clairvoyant consciousness.
What power is at work in those unlearned men who, coming over from the East, infiltrated the world of Greco-Roman culture? What power is at work in the men who bring Christianity into the foreign world of the Germanic tribes? What is really at work in the materialistic natural science of modern times – the doctrines of which disguise its real nature? What is this power? – It is Christ Himself Who, through the centuries, wends His way from soul to

soul, from heart to heart, no matter whether souls understand him or not»⁷⁵.

After these premises we should immediately specify Steiner himself has ventured, with his strong knowledge of the science of spirit, into akashic chronicles, on the traces of Jesus.

However, the founder of Anthroposophy does not report a journey of Jesus to India — he just talks, generically, about a "journey outside Palestine" — mentioning instead places where Mithras and Attis were extensively worshipped (Middle East and Persia):

«Temples dedicated to the worship of Mithras were to be found in many widely scattered regions. The rites often contained elements of the Attis cult, but were in essentials a form of Mithraic worship. Temples and centres dedicated to the worship of Mithras and Attis were numerous and widespread. It was a form of ancient heathen religion but comprised many practices and ceremonies common to Mithras or Attis worship. the fact, for example, that the Church of St. Peter in Rome stands over the site of one of these earlier places of worship shows that this cult had spread far and wide.
[…]
When in his sixteenth, seventeenth and eighteenth, Jesus of Nazareth began to journey about the country, he came to know these centres of heathen rites»⁷⁶.

---

[75] Rudolf Steiner, *The Fifth Gospel, Investigation of the Akasha Chronicle*, Rudolpf Steiner Publishing Co., London, 1950, pp. 20-21.
[76] Ivi, p. 70.

Edgar Cayce

«For all prayer is answered. Don't tell God how to answer it. Make thy wants known to Him. Live as if ye expected them to be answered. For He has given, "What ye ask in my name, believing, that will my Father in heaven give to thee"».

(Edgar Cayce)

Edgar Cayce (1877–1945) has been called the "sleeping prophet" and the most documented psychic of the 20th century.

He became very soon familiar with peculiar trance states, when he fell into a hypnotic sleep during which he was able to answer any kind of question with a competence generally considered to be much higher than his, modest, cultural level.

When he was back to his normal state of consciousness he didn't remember anything of what he told in trance and, sometimes, he didn't agree with that.

In trance, the "sleeping prophet" he diagnosed and suggested therapies, prophesied and reported suggestions from disappeared continents.

The phenomenon was reported on the pages of *New York Times* making the the psychic very popular.

He started to receive around one thousand five hundred letters every day.

Even Cayce claimed to receive information from a universal archive but, mostly, to be in contact with a voice whose messages he called "readings".
Most of them, produced within a period of over forty years, were transcribed by his stenographer.

Among the different topics the "sleeping prophet" he did not neglect the one of the journeys of Jesus.

He produced some readings with the report of three years spent by Jesus in India and his sojourns in Persia and in Egypt.

According to Edgar Cayce's readings Jesus was known everywhere with the name of Jeshua.

More specifically, in Edgar Cayce's perspective Jesus would have lived a substantial period in Benares, following the teachings of a master known as Arcahia.

Answering to the question concerning the reason why there is no mention of this phase of Jesus' life in the New Testament, Edward Cayce answered some manuscripts with crucial information have been counterfeit and the originals destroyed in Alexandria (probably together with the rest of the most important library in the ancient world).

Anne e Daniel Merois-Givaudan

Anne and Daniel Merois-Givaudan are two contemporary French writers, and are clearly "New Age oriented".

They claim in the course of two years of astral travels (or, to use a word appreciated by parapsychologists, of OOBE: *Out of body experiences*) they too consulted the annals of *Akasha*, the "prodigious memory of the universe" and, with this data collected through their non-typical means, they co-authored the book *The hidden face of Jesus from Essene memory*.

It reports detailed glimpses in to the life of Jesus and of the Essene community through the testimony of two of his pupils: Simon and Myriam.

Merois-Givaudan's book highlights a prolonged absence of Jesus from Palestine — approximately coinciding with the years the Gospels do not talk about — during which he would have lived mostly in the *Kingdom of Ishwar*: India.

The report of Jesus' stay in India, and other places (for instance Chaldea) can be read in *The hidden face of Jesus from Essene memory*, are shorter but not very different what we find in *The Aquarian Gospel*.

In the book of the two astral travellers, Jesus visits Puri, in the modern day Indian State of Orissa, where he knows the priest Lamaas, then he joins Varanasi to fight with members of higher castes and, finally, before leaving the *Kingdom of Ishwar*, he retreats for a few years to the mountains (probably the Himalayas, even if the book is not explicit in this regard).

Following this journey — through information gathered through non-standard practices — we go next to a more ordinary journey. We are still in the *Kingdom of Ishwar*, still up on the mountains and, of course, again on the trail of the great Palestinian master.

Swami Abhedananda's Journey into Kashmir and Tibet

«Of the tree of knowledge, philosophy is the flower and religion is the fruit, so they must go together.
Religion is nothing but the practical side of philosophy, and philosophy is the theoretical side of religion»[77].

(Swami Abhedanannda)

In our chorological journey we have arrived in the 1920s.

Swami Abhedananda has become the Vice-President of *Ramakrishna Math* and *Mission* of Belur Math (Kolkata), founded, in 1897, by Swami Vivekananda (1863-1902).

Swami Vivekananda had the honour of representing Hinduism in the Chicago Parliament of World Religions in 1893, resulting in him having a good reputation in the USA.

Thus when talking about Abhedananda — directly linked to Swami Vivekananda — we are talking about a member of the highest of the Indian cultural élite in the first half of the twentieth century.

Swami Abhedananda's journey into Kashmir and Tibet, from which was obtained the homonymous book, has a crucial importance.

The book basically confirms Notovitch's discovery, redeeming his reputation, which had been seriously damaged by the accusation of fraud.

As already mentioned, the book, taken from the diary of Swami Abhedananda, is not easily available today. It is self-

---

[77] *Complete works of Swami Abhedananda*, Vol. II, Ramakrishna Vedanta Math, Calcutta, 1967, p. 32.

printed by *Ramakrishna Vedanta Math*, in Kolkata and it is sold mostly in *Ramakrishna Mission*'s bookshops.

It is not easy to find it in common bookshops, in India even because it is sold at a nominal price, without offering to distributors great margins of profit.

However, I'm particularly lucky because, as I wrote, in Varanasi there is a head office of the *Ramakrishna Mission*. Therefore, I had the chance to buy several copies.

The lack of availability of the text — I've never found any quotes from it — does not make it less interesting, on the contrary, reading scrupulously *Swami Abhedananda's journey into Kashmir and Tibet* opens the door to some interesting information.

Let's start with the preface, written by Swami Prajnanananda where immediately the thesis that Jesus survived the crucifixion is presented.

It is a noteworthy factor because it has nothing to do with the manuscripts found by Notovitch, and sought after by the Swami.

This viewpoint, of Jesus having survived the crucifixion and then having journeyed to Kashmir where he died a natural death, is not linked to the Notovitch discovery. It is aligned, however, to the viewpoint of Mirzā Ghulām Ahmad.

When presenting this thesis, however, Swami Prajnanananda cites a totally difference source, referring to the previously mentioned manuscript, found in Alexandria's library: *The Crucifixion, By An Eye-Witness*.

Quoting from his preface:

«Jesus Christ, when thirty-three, was accused of heresy by the Jews in Jerusalem and capital punishment was meted out to him by the Roman ruler Pontius Pilate. He was crucified along with two other culprits. Christians believe that Jesus Christ died on the cross. But according to some historians and archaeologists Jesus did not die as a result of crucifixion.

Some of his devoted disciples rescued him from the cross in a state of unconsciousness and restored him to life through nursing and attendance. His wounds were healed through application of juice from some medicinal herbs. Accounts of these startling facts are to be found in the now-rarely available book, *The Crucifixion By An Eye-Witness*, the manuscript of which was found in Alexandria.
Many, however, hold that the facts narrated in the book are not historically correct. But there are western scholars who believe that Jesus survived his ordeal on the cross, came to India and was kept in hiding to prevent his arrest by those opposed to him. Weighty arguments are not lacking in support of this view»[78].

Then he mentions an article published on English newspaper *The Statesman* in May 1893 where there is news of another tomb of Jesus, not far from the town of Karachi in today Pakistan.

According to this extravagant thesis, the tomb was built, together with an altar, by St. Thomas (who spent — this is official — a long period in India, mostly in the area of today Tamil Nadu, where he died and is buried).

Several locals, reports the article, proudly define themselves Christian because of the conversion of their ancestors by St. Thomas.

They even claim Jesus is buried in that tomb to which people regularly offer flowers and incense while are intoned prayers, performed dances and claps of hands repeating: *victory for Jesus Christ!*
The existence of a Pakistani Christian community is coupled with the Afghan one, already considered in a former chapter, of *Followers of Jesus*.

---

[78] *Swami Abhedananda's journey into Kashmir and Tibet,* Calcutta, 1987, pp. II-III.

According to Swami Prajnanananda, however, we can get the best confirmation of Jesus' survival of the crucifixion from a Hindu source; the speech of Swami Ramatirtha: *The Spiritual Power that Wins* (*www.ramatirtha.org*).
Swami Ramatirtha has been a very prestigious figure in early twentieth-century India.
He was born in 1873 in a very poor family and in a remote village of today Pakistani Punjab.
Despite the severe state of poverty he faced with his family — being forced, sometimes, to skip meals for days — he progressed in his studies before choosing to become a Sannyasin[79] and a sort of incarnation of Vedanta.

---

[79](Sanskrit: "abandoning" or "throwing down"), in Hinduism, a religious ascetic who has renounced the world by performing his own funeral and abandoning all claims to social or family standing. *Sannyasi*s, like other sadhus, or holy men, are not cremated but are generally buried in a seated posture of meditation. Since the 5th century CE, major texts have associated this achievement with the fourth *ashrama*, or stage of life, but initially it was not so, and it is uncertain what proportion of sadhus have ever actually exemplified this ideal. According to his standard biography, even the philosopher Shankara did not, although he is often regarded as the archetypal *sannyasi*. The name *sannyasi* also designates an ascetic who pays particular allegiance to the god Shiva, especially one who belongs to the *dashanami* order said to have been established in the 8th century CE by Shankara. Among *dashanami sannyasi*s, the highest stage of achievement is recognized by the title *paramahamsa* ("great swan"). That honorific is usually given only after a probation of at least 12 years as an ascetic and only to those who have achieved full self-knowledge. They are then regarded as free of all worldly rules and duties, including formal religious obligations, and are often expected to worship internally only. Although his own practices were both Shakta (a mixture of Shaivism and local mother-goddess worship) and deeply devotional, the 19th-century saint Ramakrishna is — sometimes — regarded as a modern *paramahamsa*.

(*www.britannica.com/topic/sannyasi*)

He becomes soon very famous, traveling in Japan, the United States and Egypt.

He dies at only 33 years of age, after he has been incredibly active in a short period of time, as well as — writes Bhagwat Swarup Hony, secretary of *Swami Rama Tirtha Pratisthan* — other characters deserving the higher consideration: Adi Shankaracharya, Sant Gyaneshwar and Swami Vivekananda.

In the work, in six volumes, *In woods of God realization*, where all the speeches of Swami Ramatirtha are gathered, we can find some quotations, by Indian authorities, about him. They are also reported in the website: *www.ramatirtha.org*.

We quote, here, the most famous.

Mahatma Gandhi:
Swami Rama's teachings have got to be propagated. He was one of the greatest souls, not only of India but of the whole world. I adore his ideals.

Vinoba Bhave (A great saint, social reformer & Gandhian Philosopher):
Swami Rama Tirtha symbolized Indian spirit.

Ramana Maharshi[80]: *Swami Rama Tirtha represents True Atman.*

---

[80]«Ramana Maharshi, original name Venkataraman Aiyer, (born Dec. 30, 1879, Madurai, Madras states, India — died April 14, 1950, Tiruvannamalai), Hindu philosopher and yogi called "Great Master", "Bhagavan" (the Lord), and "the Sage of Arunachala", whose position on monism (the identity of the individual soul and the creator of souls) and maya (illusion) parallels that of Shankara (c. 700–750). His original contribution to yogic philosophy is the technique of vichara (self-"pondering" inquiry).

Born to a middle-class southern Indian Brahman family, Venkataraman read mystical and devotional literature, particularly the lives of South Indian Shaivite saints and the life of Kabir, the medieval mystical poet. He was captivated by legends of the local pilgrimage place, Mt. Aru-

Swami Shivananda (doctor-ascetic, founder of *Divine Life Society* and master of Mircea Eliade when he retired to Rishikesh, practicing yoga and ascesis and getting inspiration for his book *Yoga immortality and freedom*, a crucial work for everyone is approaching the history and philosophy of yoga): *Swami Rama Tirtha lived Practical Vedanta...He is Soul Incarnate!*

Dr. Rajendra Prasad (first President of Republic of India): *Swami Rama Tirtha was a great source of inspiration...His words go deep into the hearts of the people.*

Dr. S. Radhakrishnan (second President of Republic of India): *Swami Rama Tirtha was a Vedantin of Shankaracharya*

---

nachala, from which the god Shiva was supposed to have arisen in a spiral of fire at the creation of the world.

At the age of 17 Venkataraman had a spiritual experience from which he derived his vichara technique: he suddenly felt a great fear of death, and, lying very still, imagined his body becoming a stiff, cold corpse.

Following a traditional "not this, not that" (*neti-neti*) practice, he began self-inquiry, asking, "Who am I?" and answering, "Not the body, because it is decaying; not the mind, because the brain will decay with the body; not the personality, nor the emotions, for these also will vanish with death". His intense desire to know the answer brought him into a state of consciousness beyond the mind, a state of bliss that Hindu philosophy calls *samadhi*. He immediately renounced his possessions, shaved his head, and fled from his village to Mt. Arunachala to become a hermit and one of India's youngest gurus.

The publication of Paul Brunton's *A Search in Secret India* drew Western attention to the thought of Ramana Maharshi (the title used by Venkataraman's disciples) and attracted a number of notable students. Ramana Maharshi believed that death and evil were maya, or illusion, which could be dissipated by the practice of vichara, by which the true self and the unity of all things would be discovered. For liberation from rebirth it is sufficient, he believed, to practice only vichara and bhakti (devotion) either to Shiva Arunachala or to Ramana Maharshi».

(*www.britannica.com/biography/Ramana-Maharshi*)

order. He pronounced *Advait Vedanta* — non-Dualism — in his own fashion. His life and work will continue to guide the people!

Mrs Indira Gandhi (third Prime Minister of Republic of India, daughter of Jawahrlal Nehru):
Swami Rama Tirtha is one of the greatest saint-philosopher India has produced. We are proud of him. We should cherish his memory and try to live his Vedanta.

In Japan, Professor Takakutsu of *Tokio Imperial University*, on the occasion of Swami's visit, declared: «I have met many Pandits and Philosophers at the house of Professor Max Müller in England and other places, but I have never seen a personality like Swami Rama. In him Vedanta and Buddhism meet. He is true religion. He is a true poet and philosopher».

Even the American press did not ignore Swami's visit to the United States, in 1903, presenting him in a respectful manner.

In one of his speeches, quoted in the book *Swami Abhedananda's journey into Kashmir and Tibet*, Swami Ramatirtha expresses his opinion about some events of life of Jesus which deserves to be mentioned:

«Now, Christ regained this union with the spirit before his death. You know that Christ did not die when he was crucified. This is a fact which may be proved. He was in a state called *samadhi*, a state where all life-functions stop, where the pulse beats not, where the blood apparently leaves the veins, where all signs of life are no more, where the body is, as it were, crucified. Christ threw himself into that state for three days and like a yogi came to life again; made his escape and came back to live in Kashmir. Rama (Swami Ramatirtha) had been there and found many signs of Christ having lived there. Up to that time there was no Christian sect in Kashmir. There were many places called by his name, where

Christians never came. Cities were called by the same names as many of the cities of Jerusalem, through which Christ passed. There is standing a grave of nearly 2000 years. It is held very sacred and called the "Grave of Eash" (Isha), which is the name of Christ in Hindusthani language, and "Eash" means "prince". So there are many reasons to prove that He (Jesus) came to India, the same India where he learned his teaching»[81].

After the short and pleasant digression on Swami Ramatirtha, we consider again Swami Abhedananda's journey.
When he joins Srinagar he visits the so called tomb of Jesus in the Khana-yari district. He writes "the tomb has a sacred atmosphere" and a marvellous scent from a cavity on the wall, considered "an indication of the prophet's miraculous power".
The place, writes the Swami, is supposed to have healing powers as well.

Another belief reported by the Swami is related to a tank (known as Yusuf Talao) whose water was used by Jesus for his ablutions on the road connecting Kabul to Kashmir. It is still there and we find it mentioned in an old Arab book: *Tarik-i-Azham*.

During his visit to Khana-yari the Swami persuades himself of the authenticity of the tales about Jesus' stay in India, starting from his youth, concluding that if a research is conducted in India "the gaps in the life story of Christ can be suitably filled in"[82].

After a short stay in Srinagar, Swami Abhedananda reaches Hemis, in Ladakh, curious to see the manuscripts he read about in Notovitch's book during the long period of life (more than twenty years) he spent in the United States.

---

[81] *Swami Abhedananda's journey into Kashmir and Tibet*, op. cit., pp.III-IV.
[82] *Ivi*, p. 25.

Because of his prestigious *status*, Abhedananda has no difficulty to seeone of them, simply taken from a shelf by the lama was at his disposal in the monastery.

He tells him the manuscript contains the exact translation, in Tibetan, of an original script in the Pali language.

The Swami describes the manuscript as composed of fourteen chapters and two hundred twenty couplets (*slokas*).

He translates some fragments supported by his guiding lama and, then, he reports them on his travelogue:

«10 "Issa stepped into his thirteenth year by and by. According to the national custom of the Israelites, this is the right age for matrimony. His parents lived the life of humble folks".

11 "Their humble cottage came to be crowded with people proud of wealth and pedigree. Each of them was eager to accept Issa as his son-in-law".

12 "Issa was unwilling to marry. He had already earned the fame through his expounding the true nature of God. At the proposal of marriage he resolved to leave the house of his father in secret".

13 "At this time his great desire was to achieve full realization of God-head and learn religion at the feet of those who have attained perfection through meditation".

14 "He left Jerusalem and started on a journey to Sind in the company of a band of merchants. These merchants procured various commodities from Sind and exported the same to different lands".

***

(5)

1 "At the age of fourteen he (Jesus) crossed Sind and entered the holy land of Aryans"

2 "As he was passing all along through the land of the five rivers, his benign appearance, face radiating peace and comely forehead attracted jain devotees who knew him to be one who had received blessings from God Himself".

3 "And they requested him to stay with them in their monastery. But he turned down their request. In this time he did not like to accept anyone's service".

4 "In course of time he arrived at Jagannath Dham (Puri), the abode of Vyasa Krishna, and became the disciple of the Brahmins. He endeared himself to all and learned how to read, understand and expound the Vedas".

***

"-------After this he went on pilgrimage to Rajagriha, Benares, etc. This took six years and then he started for Kapilavastu, the place where Buddha had been born".

"-------Then he spent six years in the company of Buddhist mendicants, mastered Pali to perfection and studied all the Buddhist scriptures".

"--------From here he went to Nepal and travelled in the Himalayan region". "Then he went westwards".

"--------By and by he came to Persia, the abode of Zoroastrians" [footnote: during his journey Jesus performed ablutions at a pond and took rest for a while on its bank. The pond is still in existence and is called Isha-Talao. A fair is held every year at this spot to commemorate the incident. This matter has been described in *Tarikh-i-Azham*, a book in Arabic].

"--------His fame soon spread in all directions".

"Thus he returned to his native land once again at the age of twenty-nine. After this he started preaching his message of peace among his brethren suffering under oppression"».

The content is very similar to the one of Notovitch's book.

The Swami also writes his guiding lama told him that Jesus, after surviving crucifixion, arrived secretly in Kashmir, to live in a monastery surrounded by several pupils.

He had achieved the reputation of a great saint, attracting many people from many, different lands.

Finally, the Swami quotes the important Indian political leader Bipin Chandra Pal who reported, in one autobiographical essay, elements connecting the yogi of the Nath order with the Palestinian master.

In particular, the sacred book of the Nath reports the story of a holy man, Ishainath who had a prominent role in the transmission of the teachings of the order.

The story of Ishainath, writes the Swami quoting a passage of Bipin Chandra Pal's book, is very similar to the one of Jesus and we will consider it soon presenting another great journey done by a Chilean author: Miguel Serrano.
However, in the next chapter we will consider a third, great, traveler: the Russian painter: Nicholas Roerich.

Nicholas Roerich and the rich Himalayan oral tradition

Nikolaj Konstantinovic Roerich was born in St. Petersburg on October 10th 1874.

He has an eclectic personality, and during his lifetime (seventy-three years) he worked as painter, anthropologist, diplomat, archaeologist, poet, set designer and costume designer.

At the beginning of twentieth century he married Helena Ivanovna Shaposhnikov, nephew of the composer Modest Musorgsky. They had two sons. In 1906 he becomes Director of the *Imperial Society for the Encouragement of the Arts* in Russia and a year later designed the scenery and the costumes for Igor Stravinsky's ballet *The Rite of Spring*. He also presided, for a couple of months, over an Art Committee in the aftermath of the October revolution. Given the new, radical direction of his country, however, he decided to move on.

Since 1920 he lived in America yet after three years, he left, with the wife, for India. During this time members of the *Master Institute of United Arts* — founded by him — assembled a huge number of Roerich's works and built the *Roerich Museum*.

In 1928 he also founds the *Urusvati Himalayan Research Institute*, in Kullu valley, in India, for the study of ethnographic material and archaeological finds. In the following years, he was proposed twice — in 1929 and in 1935 — for the Nobel Prize for his commitment (through art and culture) to peace.

Roerich's wife had a strong attraction towards the esoteric knowledge and, through following this, they became members of Theosophical Society, translating one of its main texts: *The Secret Doctrine*, by Madame Blavatsky, into Russian.

Their Indian expedition, as already mentioned, started in 1923 and went on for four and a half years. During this time they visited the territories of Sikkim, Ladakh, Tibet, China and Mongolia.

The data collected during long journey was collated and recorded in the books *Himalaya*, *Altai-Himalaya* and *The heart of Asia*.

Looking for traces of the passage and stay of Jesus in those lands was one of the main motivations for the expedition.

During their journey they were able to capture and record many different oral sources and this is the main contribution the Roerichs have made to the research of "Jesus' Indian years".

Nicholas Roerich died in Kullu (Himachal Pradesh), where his ashes remain today, on the thirteenth of December 1947.

In *The heart of Asia* Roerich writes in Srinagar they had their first contact with the "curious legend" of Jesus' stay in India. During their research they were able to verify how this topic is widely known in India, in Ladakh and in Central Asia.

In particular, Roerich refers to the years not mentioned in the Gospels (the so called missing years from ages 12 to 30), but he also reports the Muslims, in Srinagar, tell them Issa didn't die on the cross, he just lost consciousness.

This relates to a post-crucifixion journey of Jesus to India.

Jesus' body was secretly treated and, once he had recovered, he has been brought to Srinagar, where he taught till he died a natural death.

In another passage of his book, Roerich writes the Muslims, in Kashmir, are deeply interested in Issa.

«Near the tomb, or Rozabal sanctuary», writes Roerich, «occur miraculous healings and the air is full of perfumes and aromas» (this is very similar to what Swami Abedhananda also reported).

The Roerichs find the legend of Jesus' visit also in Leh.

They mention an old tree, near a pond (not far from city market) under which, according to a local belief, Jesus preached to the people.

In general, the Roerichs find several versions of the same legend of a period of life spent by Jesus in India and on the Himalayas, stretching even up to Xinjiang and in Mongolia.

They are all focused on the fact that during the years not mentioned in the Gospels Jesus lived in India and in Asia.

The legends, writes Roerich in *The heart of Asia*, could have a Nestorian origin but what it is more amazing is their sincerity and genuineness.

Mentioning the area known today as Xinjiang, in *Altai-Himalaya*, Roerich writes festive anniversaries usually end with a song about Issa who, during one of his peregrinations saw a huge skull that probably belonged to a giant.

He decided to resuscitate him and the big skull began to cover itself with skin and the empty eye sockets were filled with new eyes and a large body took shape, sprayed by the blood of a big heart that begun to beat. The giant stood up thanking Issa who resuscitated him for the good of all of humanity.

Even among the Calmocks, writes Roerich, it is possible to find the "legend of Issa" which corresponds to the one of the manuscripts found by Notovitch..

It is very likely, Roerich concludes, it did not penetrate in Calmucchia, lapped to the South by the Caspian sea, from Hemis' monastery and it has, probably, a different origin.

And now, after I have offered a summary of the discoveries of the Roerichs, I will give provide a report of another journey. This is an account of a journey I personally made in the Punjab, enriched by a quick historical introduction.

Qadian 15-29/12/2014

On the eighth of April 1336, in Kesh (known today as Shahrisabz, in Uzbekistan), was born Timur Barlas, also known as Temur-i Lang (Tamerlane).

His birth-place is not far from the famous City of Samarcanda — an important junction on the Silk Road where the Greek and Indian worlds met and influenced each other.

Later in his life he chose Samarcanda as both the capital of his empire and, in 1405, as his final burial place.

The renowned Timurid Empire took root in Persia and Central Asia, up to part of Northern India, and was administered by the homonymous dynasty.

Considered as the last great nomad conqueror of Eurasian steppes, Tamerlane self-identified as "the sword of Islam" and the heir of Gengis Khan.

The Timurid empire, where was born also Zahir-ud-din Muhammad Babur — descendant of Tamerlane through his paternal line and Gengis Khan via his maternal one — founder of the Mughal empire in India, was soon, culturally, Persianised. Indeed, Persian culture has dominated Central Asia since the beginning of the Islamic expansion.

Members of Persian dominant classes, boasting a lineage from important leaders and conquerors started to title themselves as Amīrzāde: son of the commander.

The word, in fact, is composed of the Arabic title *Amir* (related to the Semitic root Amr): to command combined with the Persian suffix *zād*: meaning birth or lineage.

It is probably more familiar to us the word Emir, deriving from *Amir*: the title used by Tamerlane, who could not use either Khan's — because he was not fully descended from

Gengis Khan — nor Khalifa's — because he was not a member of *Quraysh's* tribe (the one of Prophet Muhammad) from which started the Islamic caliphate lineage.

From *Amir* and *Amīrzāde* derives the noble title of Mirza, conferred by kings, sultans and emperors to children, grandchildren, relatives and nobles deemed worthy.

With the beginning of the Mughal empire in India, in the first half of the sixteenth century, the title arrived in South Asia that is culturally influenced by Persia, particularly in the large areas conquered by Islam.

All the Mughal emperors, starting from the aforementioned founder Ẓahīr ud-Dīn Muhammad (1483-1530), better known as Babur, had the title of Mirza.

During Babur's reign there arrived in India (precisely in Punjab) — from Samarcanda — Mirza Hadi Baig, a candidate scholar to be the first *qadi* (a judge responsible for the correct application of sharia's dictates) of the area. The first Mughal emperor granted him the jurisdiction over 80 Punjabi villages. Mirza Haid Baig called the local administrative centre Islam Pur Qazi and it is from this name that later would be derived the name Qadian.

In the following years, after several changes of power (benefitting, at the beginning, the Sikhs and then, in the second half of the nineteenth century, the British), the descendants of Mirza Haid Baig lost the jurisdiction over the villages and the administrative centre, while remaining its most important exponents.

As mentioned previously, in 1889 Mirzā Ghulām Ahmad — great-grandson of Mirza Haid Baig — established, in Qadian, the *Ahmadiyya Muslim Community*.

Then the town becomes the capital of *the Ahmadiyya Caliphate* until 1947, the date of the independence of India and of the birth — unfortunately not bloodless — of Pakistan, where moved the Community (led by Mirza members) till a later change in circumstance required another transfer, this time to London[93].

However, Qadian is still today the "holy town" of Ahmadiyya Community, annually hosting a *Jalsa Salana*, one of main international meetings of the Community.

After this introduction, I go back to my travelogue and the story of my experience in the field.

***

I arrive in Qadian late in the evening.

It is approximately 9.00 p.m. and the roads are almost entirely empty.

The bus station is an unpaved and desolate square where the wind moves litter and light trash.

I don't see any taxi or tuk-tuk or rickshaw.

Aijaz phoned me a couple of hours ago, to be sure I was on the right way.

The train from Varanasi to Amritsar arrived with a severe delay and from the Sikh's holy town it took a couple of hours to reach Qadian.

However, I've another telephone number, of Mr. Nasim Khan and I use it.

When he's informed there are no taxi or tuk-tuk or rickshaw nearby, he asks me to pass the phone to a local person.

There is a small garage a few steps from me.

I ask to the boy working there, who is already looking at me with the usual "Indian curiosity", to talk with my interlocutor.

---

[93]For further information please read the article, in the Appendix: *Ahmadiyya Muslim Community; for a violence-free Islam.*

He is very happy to do it.

They have a very short conversation then the boy, giving me back my cell phone, tells me: «My brother will drop you there on his motorbike, you are not far!».

«Thank you!», I answer.

«Welcome, *As Salaam-Allaikum!*[94]»

«*As Salaam-Allaikum*», I answer confused and giving the wrong answer.

Indeed the right answer should be *Wa-Alaikum-Salaam*[95] but I have to get used to the new greeting.

In the first days in Qadian I will often slip up using the peculiar hindu greeting *Namasté*[96] (after the pleasant "Varanasian quarantine"...).

However my hosts, although not such, will have no objections.

I jump on the "salvific" motorbike.

The driver goes through narrow alleys.

The small town is quite compact and reminds me an Italian 16th century village on the plain.

We arrive soon at the Headquarters of *Ahmadiyya Muslim Community*. This is also quite compact, with a wide, central courtyard, two floors of rooms for guests side by side on Spartan balconies.

I ask again about Nasim but he is not there. I'm rather requested to enter in one office, very near the entry gate.

A middle aged man, in charge there, invites me to sit on a swivel chair. I have to wait around twenty minutes before he can attend to me, he is indolently finishing a discussion with another person.

---

[94] Traditional Muslim greeting. It could be synthetically translated, from Arabic, with: peace (of God) be upon you!
[95] "Peace be upon you as well!".
[96] Literally: I bow down to you!

Jalsa Salana, the yearly gathering of Ahmadiyya Community, is approaching and I know I would have found a busy environment.

I'm quite tired and slightly cold even if in the office I can enjoy the soft warmth of an electric heater. I'm then asked to reach the near, intimate refectory.

«Now eat», the *receptionist* tells me, «the room is ready and make yourself comfortable, you have arrived home!».

«I know!», I answer instinctively.

I eat some good mutton's meat and I'm glad, immediately after, to reach my room.

The room is big and welcoming even if not luxury. It has four beds, two single and a double one.

There is no heating system. The town has a very damp climate and the bed sheets are almost wet.

I've my own blanket but other ones are there available to guests.

I go straight to bed, enjoying a documentary on my *laptop*.

The day after I'm in the office of Nasim Khan, not far from the guesthouse where I'm accommodated.

The Community headquarters are distributed in several buildings and the main one is the fortified citadel of Mirzā Ghulām Ahmad's family where there is also a big mosque and an high, white minaret with a high symbolic meaning[97]. In the citadel there is also a small bank whose bank account holders don't get and don't pay any interest.

---

[97] As we considered about the mainstream Islamic eschatology, it is believed that when Jesus will return to earth to inaugurate forty years of perfect Muslim life, he will come down from the white minaret of the Umayyad Mosque in Damascus. In the case of the Ahmadiyya Islamic Community, the presence of the white minaret in its mosques recalls this mythical motif. However, in Ahmadiyya perspective, as it as already mentioned, the messianic figure is Mirza Ghulam Ahmad, already arrived on earth in an "ordinary" manner.

Nasim Khan is the *Director of Internal Affairs* of the Community and he welcomes me warmly. He knows about my publishing project and he intends to involve a guy who could assist me.

He joins us a few minutes later. His name is Zabi Ullah, he is twenty-three years old, he is an IT engineer and he will be a sort of sober guardian angel during my stay in Qadian.

We start our work immediately

He takes me to the community library, then to another complex where the Ahmadiyyas have their own publishing house, their own recording studio, rooms for conferences and meetings, and more.

The people in charge of the publishing house donate to me several copies of books related to my research. They also provide me with one copy of the Holy Quran in Italian.

Indeed, one of the Ahmadiyya cultural projects is the translation of the holy book of Islam in seventy-two different languages.

My permanence among the Ahmadiyya will become a full immersion in their being Muslims and, to a lesser extent, in Islam in general.

I soon realise my serious gaps in the knowledge of a world that has made an incredibly profound contribution to the history of the last fourteen centuries.

The days at Qadian will pass intensely — sometimes punctuated with practical problems — and enlightening.

I will appreciate the versatile politeness of my hosts, I will discover stories of ancient aristocracies, unusual angles on our Christian world and its founder, different ways of being Ahmadiyya, relating, during the Jalsa Salana, with Kyrgyz, Nigerian, Palestinian, Indonesian and many Pakistani followers.

In the course of many evenings, huddled under my blanket, drying the damp sheets with the warmth of my body, I will go, with due discretion, into the Koranic suras. I will participate in a spontaneous fraternal agape, sharing a lunch of fried chicken.

We will all get the food, with our hands, from the same overflowing dishes, without any individualistic narrow-mindedness of any kind, and I will thus have the opportunity to rediscover the noble freshness of the original Christianity.

I will read, I will photocopy, I will proceed in the search, I will get precious contacts to carry it forward in other lands, I will meditate comfortably sitting on the soft carpet of a semi-desert mosque, assimilating for a few moments the etymological meaning of the term Islam: peace and submission (or, as I prefer: surrender), feeling the good resonance with the Ahmadiyya slogan: love for all, hatred for none.

I leave Qadian on a sunny afternoon, for a comfortable hotel in Amritsar and other sheets damp to shake.

Zabi Ullah accompanies me on his motorcycle to the bus station, with the suitcase badly stuck between our bodies.

The bus is already roaring in the dirt and desolate station.

I have to catch it quickly, there is no time for long greetings.

After all, there is nothing to say but "thank you!".

"Thanks to you!", replies Zabi Ullah, without losing his sobriety.

I leave Qadian with contained emotion, grateful for having had a small-great cognitive opportunity and having briefly seen the world with other eyes.

Miguel Serrano; from the Andes to the Himalayas on the trail of the Siddha Ashram

I found Miguel Serrano's *The serpent of paradise* quoted, in *The fifth gospel*, by Maria Fida Hassnain.

It is a text now out of print, the first edition is from 1963.

I've looked for it in India, in libraries and bookstores, without success.

I've found it in the *Shaman Bookshop*, a bookstore in Chiang Mai (in northern Thailand), probably the best one in the town, run by a bookseller of other times.

There is an atmosphere reminiscent of the seventies, informal and veracious, in *Shaman Bookshop*.

Then, it is a place for amateurs where you can find the result of efforts spanning many decades, in which books have been extracted from many cellars and attics by the expert eye of the bookseller.

When I crossed the threshold of the Shaman Bookshop I knew I would find what I was looking for.

The serpent of paradise, today, is a book for collectors.

It is the story of a meeting of a westerner — Miguel Serrano himself, from Chile — with India before the country was invaded by Western travellers, hippies, hashish smokers, and so on.

I think *The serpent of paradise; the story of an Indian pilgrimage* represents a middle way between Mircea Eliade's Indian Travel Diary (where he describes the country at the end of the twenties, still under the colonial yoke) and the vulgar *Indian journals* by Allen Ginsberg which projects us in the phase of the fashion, in my opinion a bit trivial, of journeying in India.

The India that emerges from the pages of *The serpent of paradise* is explicitly crude. The images that Serrano offers us are, often, terrifying but deep. Indeed they are due to the reflections of a person who, in a country culturally very far from his own, tries to make a constant empathic effort not to lose the awareness of the radicality and significance of that difference. At the same time, the author doesn't reject Indian magical and mystical dimension even according to his clear, cultural familiarity with the magical world. From this point of view, Serrano's book is reminiscent of the ones of his countryman Alejandro Jodorowsky (I had the chance to know him in Paris where he read the tarot at *Café Le Temeraire*).

In *The serpent of paradise* we find an India explored without rush and in solitary depth, in a period when very few westerners ventured there, with a precise goal. However it is not unusual, in India (even today), to forget "the precise goal". It can be easily lost in the meanders of a journey that, with its pregnancy, in many ways transcends it. Serrano, in fact, will miss, in India, the place he was searching for: the Himalayan *Siddha Ashram* where he could have discovered the initiatory lineage of his Chilean master[98] but he will find several other things. For instance the Kashmiri version of Jesus' story, to which he dedicates a chapter of his book.

He writes:

«While there are tales of Christ's childhood and of his visit to the temple, there is virtually no information concerning his life during his young manhood. Nobody knows what he did or where he lived until he was thirty, the year when he began his preaching.
There is a legend, however, that says that he was in Kashir, the original name for Kashmir. *Ka* means "the same as" or "equal to" and *shir* means Syria. Manuscript in the Sharda language, which is

---

[98] The author is quite generic about this.

derived from Sanskrit, seem to bear close relationship to the biblical story. According to this Kashmiri legend, Jesus came to Kashir and studied under holy men, who taught him mysterious signs. These had been preserved intact in the high mountains which had not been inundated by the flood. Among these may have been the science of Nila, the king of serpents. Later Jesus returned to the Middle East and he then began to preach among the ignorant masses of Israel the mystical truths he had learned in Kashir. To impress and to convert them, he often used the powers he had acquired through the practice of Yoga and these were then referred as miracles. Then in due course Jesus was crucified, but he did not die on the cross. Instead, he was removed by some Essene brothers, restored to good health and sent back to Kashir, where he lived with his masters until his natural death.

There is some evidence which suggests that this legend is Islamic in origin, but it is probably even older. In ancient times there was much traffic between India and the Middle East, and it is very likely that the stories and myths of India were carried across the desert into the Holy Land. Certainly the myth of the crucifixion of a redeemer is of enormous antiquity, and the concept of the equality of all men had already been preached by Buddha and was carried into Kashmir by King Ashoka long before Jesus began to preach to the fishermen.

A number of investigations have also been made concerning a tomb which is to be found in Srinagar, and which is said to be the tomb of Jesus. It is possible, of course, that this is merely the tomb of an old Islamic saint or of a Sufi master, for there is nothing really precise in these speculations. I myself have seen this tomb, although very few people know about it and it is difficult to find.

[…]

It was evening when I first arrived at the tomb, and in the light of the sunset the faces of the men and children in the street looked almost sacred. They looked like people of ancient times; possibly they were related to one of the lost tribes of Israel that are said to have migrated to India. The children were wearing long shirts and primitive jewels, and their eyes were very bright.

The building containing the tomb was just at the corner of a square. Taking off my shoes, I entered and found a very old tomb surrounded by a filigree stone fence which protected it, while to one side there was the shape of a footprint cut into the stone. It is said to be the footprint of Yousa-Asaf, and according to the legend, Yousa-Asaf is Jesus.

On the wall of the building hangs an inscription, and below it a translation from the Sharda into English. This inscription reads:

    Yousa-Asaf (Khanya, Srinagar)

The description written below is copied from a book kept in Astana.

When he wrote the short description of the place called Sved Nazair-Udin-Mir, Khanyara of Wakiat-Kashmiri, the famous historian of Kahmir called Khaja Mohammed Azan Dechmarij, declared the following: All the people say that there was a prophet who came to Kashmir a long time ago. That time was called the time of the prophets. In another part of this short description, entitled Wakiati-Kashmir, the historian says: One of the main princes who came to Kashmir and who prayed here a great deal, night and day, was Yousa-Asaf. His tomb is located near Aunzimed, in Khanya Mutwa Nazair-ud-mir Rozaball Khanyar»[99].

Surely even Serrano, in a suggestive manner, adds another, even vague, piece.

He writes about manuscripts in Sharda language that, maybe, could be found and studied.

He mentions an inscription, in Rozabal, who has disappeared and a historian who could be better known.

In short, even in this case we certainly didn't get incontrovertible proofs of Jesus' stay in India but some inspiration

---

[99]Miguel Serrano, *The serpent of paradise, the story of an Indian pilgrimage*, RKP, London, 1974, pp. 62-63.

that can be a starting point for a subsequent, more structured research.

Proceeding in writing his book, Serrano mentions Jewish migration in India.

The first, quite important, one dates back, in his analysis, to the second destruction of Jerusalem temple, in 70 AD and it involved the territory of today Kerala.

Serrano claims that, in general, the Jewish people were known as Anjuvarnar: the fifth caste (in addition to the four castes of Hindu tradition: Brahmins[100], Kshatrya[101], Vaysya[102] and Shudra[103]).

After some digressions, Serrano proposes an interesting thesis.

He writes in Cochin — Kerala — (the author, ambassador in India between 1953 and 1962, offers data from the fifties and sixties) there were two Jewish communities living in different areas and frequenting two different synagogues.

The two communities were known as the one of "black Jewish" — similar to black Dravidians, according to Serrano's thesis they have reached India immediately after the destruction of the Temple — and the one of "white Jewish", who would have arrived in India in more recent times and whose houses recalled Seventeenth century Dutch architectural style.

The white Jewish, writes Serrano, claimed the "black" ones didn't arrive after the Temple's destruction done by the Romans.

In this case, writes the Chilean author, we should consider other explanations and hypothesis, for instance they were

---

[100] The depositaries of sacred knowledge.
[101] Warriors.
[102] Traders.
[103] Simple workers.

natives of India and they converted to the religion of Abraham.

However, we know it is not easy to convert to Judaism and, for this reason, Serrano considers another hypothesis that is the Jewish race has and Indian origin, Dravidian to be precise.

As well as the gypsies they moved, in ancient times, to the West, keeping their own ethnic specificity intact, avoiding the hybridisation probably because of their memory of the caste system.

The theory of the "Indian origins" of the Jewish people is quite coherent, writes Serrano, with the hypothesis of Indian stay of Jesus, corroborated even by his claim to be the son of God.

The concept of "divine incarnation", write Serrano — and, as we have considered before, Swami Abhedananda — has had a kind of "honorary citizenship", in India, for centuries.

Then, Serrano mentions the manuscripts found by Notovitch we have already abundantly considered.

He also considers another "curious manuscript" which has been already mentioned, *Nath Namavali Sutra*, preserved among the sadhus of Yoga Nath, "in the Vindhya range of mountains", in the Indian State of Uttar Pradesh, not far from Benares.

In the manuscript it is written Jesus-Ishai Nath reached India when he was fourteen years old. After about sixteen years of asceticism he concluded that Shiva was the supreme divinity, he came back to his own country where he started to preach up to incurring the conspiracy of his countrymen and being crucified. Even in the Nath version he survived the cruel ordeal, entering a state of Samadhi, accessible to advanced practitioners of yoga.

One of the guru of Nath tradition supported him: Chetan Nath, able to make his body "lighter than air", reaching the lands of Israel along with the roar of thunder and lightning and earth tremor.

Chetan Nath took Ishai Nath's body from the grave, awakening it from the state of Samadhi and then bringing it back to the "lands of the Aryans" in India. Ishai Nath would have founded an ashram in the lower Himalayan areas, perhaps in Kashmir, establishing a peculiarly Shiva cult.

When he was forty nine he left his body after he got the full control of it through yoga practices.

Serrano concludes by reporting the song of the yogi, sung by the Nath, in which are mentioned Jesus and John the Baptist:

«My friend, to what country did Ishai go, and to what country went John?
My friend, where is the *guru* of the *gurus*, and where is your mind resting?
My friend, Ishai has gone towards Arabia, John towards Egypt.
My friend, Ishai is the *guru* of my *gurus*. The mind of the yogi rests only in the Yogi»[104].

---

[104]*Ivi*, p. 79.

The Rajneesh Bible and the Pilate's letter to Tiberius

«It was [...] neither Tiberius nor Pilate who condemned Jesus. It was the old Jewish party; it was the Mosaic law.
[...]
Now, if ever a crime was the crime of a nation, it was the death of Jesus. This death was "legal" in the sense that it was primarily caused by a law which was the very soul of the nation.
The Mosaic law, it is true, in its modern, yet accepted form, pronounced a penalty of death against all attempts to change the established worship.
Now, there is no doubt that Jesus attacked this worship, and hoped to destroy it. The Jews espressed this to Pilate with truthfull simplicity: "we have a law, and by our law he ought to die; because he has made himself the Son of God". The law was detestable, but it was the law of ancient ferocity; and the hero who attempted to abrogate it, had first of all to endure its penalty»[107].

«It is evident [...] that doubts arose a sto the reality of the death of Jesus. A few hours' suspension on the cross appeared to persons in the habit of seeing crucifixions quite insufficient to bring about such a result. They quoted many instances of crucified persons, who, having been removed in time, had been restored to life by powerful remedies. Origen, at a later date, thought it necessary to invoke miracle in order to explain so sudden an end»[108].

In the last Palestinian events of the life of Jesus and in front of his suspected death, Pilate — who, according to

---

[107]Ernest Renan, *The life of Jesus*, The Temple Company, London, 1888, pp. 176-177.
[108]Ernest Renan, *The life of Jesus*, Walter Scott LTD, London, 1898, p. 269.

what is reported in the *Gospel of Mark*[109], was the first to be marvelled because of it — may have played a more important role than one might think.

After all it is quite suspicious Jesus, unlike the two crucified thieves on his right and left sides, didn't have his legs broken (the practice is known as *crurifragium* and it was used to accelerate the death of people put on the cross).

It is also legittimate to consider anomalous body of Jesus has been given — without any objection from the Roman prefect[110] — to Joseph of Arimathea and Nicodemus.

Over time, therefore, various hypotheses emerged identifying, in some cases, Pilate as a "accomplice" of a plan designed to save, even *in extremis*, Jesus from death.

Andreas Faiber-Kaiser, author of *Gesù vise e morì in Kashmir* (*Jesus lived and died in Kashmir*), quotes a letter Pilate, according to Christian Apocrypha Pilate Cylce, wrote to Tiberius.

In that letter Pilate does not hide his sympathies for the Pastinian teacher.

The letter is quite short and the nit can be fully quoted:

«Pontius Pilate to the Emperor Tiberius Caesar greeting.

On Jesus Christ, of whom I told you clearly in my last letter, a cruel punishment has been inflicted by the will of the people. I was unwilling and apprehensive about it. He was a man, by Hercules, so pious and upright no age has ever had nor will ever have. But the efforts of the people themselves, and the unanimity of all the scribes, chiefs and elders to crucify this ambassador of truth, were remarkable, even though their prophets, like the Sibyls with us,

---

[109]«Pilate marveled that He was already dead; and summoning the centurion, he asked him if He had been dead for some time» (Mark, 15/44).

[110]Quoting the respective Gospel passage: «So when he found out from the centurion, he granted the body to Joseph» (Mark, 15/45).

warned against it. Supernatural signs appeared when he was hanging, and in the judgement of philosophers these threatened the destruction of the whole world. His disciples flourish, and in their work and temperate life they did not belie their master, but rather in his name they are most beneficent.

Had I not greately feared an uprising of the people, who were on the point of rebelling, that man would perhaps still be alive for us. Constrained more by fidelity to your dignity than led by my own will, I did not strive to the utmost of my power to prevent the loss and suffering of righteous blood, guiltless of every accusation.

It was an injustice due to the malice of men, although, as the scriptures testify, it was to their own destruction.

Farewell

The Fifth of the Kalends of April»[111].

The Essene author of the letter quoted in *The Crucifixion, By An Eye-Witness* proposes a less idyllic version: Pilate would have been an accomplice in the plan to save Jesus simply because he was bribed. Then, according to this hypothesis, once he was paid, he agreed to give Jesus' body to Joseph of Arimathea without subjecting it to *crurifragium*.

Osho Rajneesh (1931-1990) — a particularly controversial Indian master who, I think, does not need to be introduced — in one of his speeches, quoted in the book *The Rajneesh Bible*, goes ahead.

He claims Pilate was totally involved in the plot, being completely convinced it was right to save Jesus' life.

Quoting directly his words:

«Judea was under the Romans, and Pontius Pilate was the governor general, the viceroy of Rome in Judea. Pontius Pilate had

---

[111] Elliott J.K., *The Apocryphal New Testament*, Clarendon Press, Oxford, 1993, pp. 207-208.

nothing against Jesus. At the most he thought him a some-what hot-blooded young man, which is very natural; that's how a young man should be. But he had not committed any crime, he had not induced anybody else to commit any crime; and to put him on the cross, which is the ultimate punishment you give to murderers, seems to be absolutely illogical. And he was a cultured man. He tried to persuade the high priest of the Jews that, "I don't see what crime this man has committed [...]".
[...]
And to me Pilate was perfectly right.So he and a rich follower of Jesus conspired the whole plot. He wanted this young man to be freed.
[...]
And this was a simple arrangement: that the crucifixion should happen on Friday, thatit should be delayed as much as possible — so almost on Friday afternoon.
[...]
So this was the conspiracy: that by the evening, when the sun sets, he will not be dead; he was only on the cross for six hours.
Nobody has ever died on the Jewish cross in six hours. Twenty-four hours, thirty-six hours, forty-eight hours, people have even taken sixty hours to die. And what was the strategy? Because Saturday is the Sabbath, everything stops for the Jews; no work can be done. And the body of Jesus has to be brought down from the cross after six hours, because the sun is setting; now all work stops. So he was perfectly alive; he had just lost a little blood. He never died on the cross.
[...]
Jesus is taken down from the cross, put into a cave, with a big rock as a door so he cannot escape – because the people who brought him down knew perfectly well that he is alive. Even in the Bible it is reported that one soldier poked his sword in his side and blood came out. Blood does not come out of a dead man; he was just making sure that he was alive. And in the night he was removed from there. Now it will be only on the Monday morning

that the cave door will be opened – and the cave was found empty. Jesus escaped from Jerusalem[112].

Also Osho identifies Kashmir as the final place where Jesus, fleeing from his executioners, arrived and where he died and was buried. However, he oddly identified a different tomb from the very famous one of Rozabal's shrine.
The tomb Osho spoke about should be beside "the Musa one".
"On the grave", Osho claimed, should be visible the name Joshua who, it should be written, "came here, lived here to the ripe age of one hundred and twelve years, died here. And in his memory we have changed the name of the place"[113].
The name given to the place which has been maintained till today is Pahalgam: "The village of the shepherd".

This is the first thesis I found about "Indian years of Jesus" and it has fascinated me.
In August 2015 I've spent around ten days in Pahalgam, not far from Srinagar where, by now, I feel almost at home.
Of course I've looked for the close tombs of Jesus and Musa but without success.
Somebody claims they are in an area where today there is a small church, on a small piece of fenced and inaccessible land.
I have tried to investigate with several people but nobody was supporting the hypothesis of Osho in Pahalgam.
But there are several supporters of the presence of tomb of Moses in Kashmir; for instance Maria Fida Hassnain, Faiber Kaiser, Ahmadiyya authors and Holger Kersten.

---

[112]Osho Rajneesh, *The Rajneesh Bible*, Rajneesh Foundation International, Rajneeshpuram, Oregon (USA)Vol I, 1985, p. 104.
[113]*Ivi*, p. 112.

However it should be not in Pahalgam but not far from a Kashmiri small town: Bandipur, around sixty kilometers from Srinagar, in the opposite direction to Pahalgam.

I've ventured on those mountains, till Both, the village where, according to a map on Faiber Kaiser's book, there should ne the resting place of the famous prophet.

When I reached the place, getting some information by the shepherds about the presence of a *Musa Mosque* at the end of Both, I'm kept in custody for about half an hour by some guarding soldiers (the area is particularly sensitive, not far from famous LOC — *Line of Control* — on the border between India and Pakistan). Then I got the permission to see the place where the supposes Moses' tomb share a beautiful grassy pitch with the ones of three Muslim saints.

Actually, the space is occupied by two simple gabled mausoleums and a bigger one, where is buried Sank Bibi, "a renowned hermitess [...] who excelled men in meditation and prayers"[114]. They are all green painted (the sacred color of Islam) — and with green drapes on the stone sarcophagi — and open but there is no mention of the prophet for whom I'd done a long (fortunately pleasant) all uphill walk.

I had short time for visit and I couldn't do it quietly, constantly escorted by a group of vociferous children.

But it is touching for me the memory of that rarefied air, the scent of resin, the magico f the beginning of the evening with a view on a wide valley embellished by a lake, the faces framed in veils of delicate pastel color of young women on their way back to the village while I was leaving it. Their gazes discreet, austere and, perhaps, inexorably sad.

---

[114]Kashmiri Aziz, *Christ in Kashmir*, Srinagar, Roshni Publications, 1984, p. 43.

It was the first of May, I don't know if I will have the chance, in future, to live another International Worker's Day of the same intensity.

Going back, shortly, on the Golgotha, among the skeptics about the lethal outcome of the crucifixion we find also the Italian satirical author Jacopo Fo, son of famous Dario Fo: actor, playwright, comedian, singer, theatre director, songwriter, painter, political campaigner for the Italian left wing and the recipient of the 1997 Nobel Prize in Literature.

Jacopo Fo wrote, in 2000, a book with an ironic and provocative title — *Gesù amava le donne e non era biondo (Jesus loved women and was not blond)* — where he also highlights Jesus remained on the cross three, maximum six hours; a time generally considered insufficient to die.

In this regard, he supports a particularly fitting argument. Probably few people know in the Philippines, during the Easter period, some Catholic penitents, in compliance with a particularly demanding vote, are crucified with nails and ropes.

It is possible to find some videos, frankly a bit shocking, on You Tube (for instance the BBC documentary: *Did Jesus die on the cross* where it is possible to see images of short crucifixions in the Philippines).

Quoting the translation of a short passage from Jacopo Fo's book:

«In the evening the penitents are removed from the cross and treated and they, of course, do not die»[115].

Even the Shroud, writes again Fo, could be considered a valid proof Jesus survived the crucifixion:

---

[115]Jacopo Fo, *Gesù amava le donne e non era biondo (Tutto quello che non ti dicono a catechismo)*, Edizione Nuovi Mondi, Alcatraz (PG), 2000, p. 118.

«Dr. Kittermaster (a pathology specialist in Tunbridge Wells, UK) [...] claims that the traces of blood at the wound to the side show that Jesus was alive at the time of the deposition from the cross because blood does not come out of a dead body. The flowing blood shows the cardiac activity»[116].

...But we will consider the Shroud in a next chapter. May the Buddhist virtue of patience accompany you!

---

[116]*Ivi*, p. 119.

Other bibliographical contributions about the Indian years of Jesus

As I have written at the beginning of this book, after the pioneering work done by Nicholas Notovitch and Mirza Ghulām Ahmad, the controversial issue of possible Indian years of Jesus became the subject of a wide debate. Then we are going to share some other reflections proposing, first of all, a theroretical grid which could represent a stable reference for most of the people interested in the hypothesis of our research.

We will focus on the hypothesis of Nicholas Notovitch and Mirza Ghulām Ahmad (and respective followers). Regarding the esoteric approach, even maintaining a possibilist attitude, I temporarily suspend all judgment:

A) In general it is very important to highlight, as a crucial prerequisite for the likelihood of both the hypothesis of Nicholas Notovitch and Mirza Ghulām Ahmad, that the connections between the Middle East and India, at Jesus' time, were con-spicuous;

B) Nicholas Notovitch, unlike Mirza Ghulām Ahmad, claims Jesus spent several years in India in the long period of his life not reported in the Gospels: between thirteen and thirthy years;

C) Mirza Ghulām Ahmad, instead, claims Jesus went to India in the years following his crucifixion to which he survived. Within this second perspective several people (mostly followers of Mirza Ghulām Ahmad) did and continue to do even today massive researches. Then, in this case, we can dispose of some written documents of Hindu and Muslim background.

D) Within this second perspective it is claimed that the Afghan and Kashmiri peoples are in large part of Jewish origin. The reason of these ethnic ties is related with the several diasporas suffered by the Jews since Assyrian occupation.

The presence of descendants of ten lost tribes of Israel in Afghanistan and Kashmir should be one of the main reasons of Jesus' stay in those lands after the ordeal of crucifixion.

Documented presence of *Followers of Jesus*, in Afghanistan, represents a particularly interesting element supporting this hypothesis;

E) The perspective of Mirza Ghulām Ahmad and those who have followed his reasearch is connected to the studies on the presumed tomb of Jesus in Srinagar and on the Shroud; on the linen which should have wrapped an alive body instead of a corpse. The same body should have been buried in *Rozabal*'s mausoleum. The supporters of this perspective press for a comparative study of DNA of the man buried in *Rozabal* and the one whose body has been wrapped in the Shroud's linen.

We can start focusing on the first point, reconsidering the crucial role of famous Silk Route and quoting, again, Indian Nobel prize winner Amartya Sen:

«One of the dominant influences in understanding the contact and intercourse between Asia and Europe is the impact and influence of what is called the Silk Route. Extending over 4000 miles, this was the route through which merchandise moved between Asia and Europe. Silk was one of the principal exports of China — hence the name. Originally established between the third century

BC and the third century AD, during the Han Dynasty, the Silk Route was of profound importance not only for trade and commerce, but also for intermingling of people and ideas.
[…]
If trade gets people together (and it certainly does), then so does interest in knowledge and enlightenment. Mathematics, science, engineering and the arts, along with religious and ethical commitments, have moved the people across regions, by land and across the seas, in pursuit of human interest in them.
The important point is that the motivation behind these journeys was not the pursuit of commercial gains, but search for ideas.
The huge popularity of seeing global connections only through the prism of trade, of which the Silk Route is a leading example, should not be allowed to eclipse the fact that reflective engagements have also moved people across countries and regions over millennia»[117].

Again about the depth and the meaningfulness of relations between East and West — strongly diluted after the crusades and the consequent deep division between the Christian and the Islamic worlds and, then, re-established some centuries later but mostly under the colonialism's aegis — we cannot ignore the exceptional adventure of Alexander the Great (356-323 BC).

Indeed it has created the presuppositions for the establishment of a huge supranational empire whose peoples and cultures deeply influenced each others. Then followed the Diadochi's reigns, allowing a more stable and fruitful exchange among individuals of different ethnic and cultural origins.

In the Hellenistic world spread Eastern religions because of the alternate movement of Asiatic people (traders, slaves, soldiers, etc.) toward the West, along with their heritage of

---

[117]In: Amartya Sen, *The country of the first boys*, Oxford University Press, New Delhi, 2015, pp. 254-255.

traditional gods and of Western people toward the East where they knew new forms of worship and new divinities.

The result was an interesting range of syncretisms.

The most of religious and cultural patterns arrived in the West from Egypt, Asia Minor, Syria and Persia but we know Alexander the Great reached the land of five rivers (the territories of today Punjab) and that later the relations among his successors and the élites of contemporary Indian kingdoms, mostly with the Magadha (corresponding to today Indian state of Bihar), have been intense, as we can deduce from the book *Indika*, authored by the Greek historian Megasthes (c. 350 BC – c. 290 BC), ambassador to the Chandragupta Maurya court in Pataliputra (today Patna), the capital of Magadha.

The same Kingdom was invaded, in the second century BC, by Menander I — general ofthe army of Greek king of Bacrtia (today Afghanistan) Demetrius — "the first Greek conqueror to cross Beas river, succeeding where even Alexander failed"[118].

However, even Menander I had to give up his venture a short time later but he soon inherited from Demetrius — remembered by the Latin historian Justin as *Rex Indorum* for the brave venture beyond the Beas river of his general — the sovereignty over north-west India.

Menander, writes Stephen Batchelor in his excellent book *The awakening of the West*, "proved to be the most successful of all Greek rulers in India, renowned as a brilliant general and administrator, as well as a man of great intellectual sensitivity"[119].

He is the only Indo-Greek king present in Indian literature and in the western literature of Plutarch, and represents, in

---

[118]Stephen Batchelor, *The awakening of the West. The encounter of Buddhism and Western culture*, HarperCollins, London, 1994, p. 12.
[119]*Ibidem*.

the perspective of Batchelor, "a synthesis of Alexander and Ashoka, a person who was both a Greek hero and a Buddhist king"[120].

«For Indians the outstanding memory of Menander is that he alone among the Greek kings adopted Buddhism.
One of the best-known texts in Pali (also preserved in Chines) is the *Milindapañha* (*Menander's Questions*), the record of a dialogue between the king and a Buddhist monk called Nāgasena.
The precise extent of Menander's commitment to Buddhism is open to question. Although the Pali text concludes in declaring how Menander renounced the world, became a monk and attained the state of an arhat, a more credible outcome is suggested by the king himself:

"As a lion captured in a golden cage stretches its neck outwards, even so do I, while remaining in the world, aspire for solitude. But if I left the world to take up the religious life, I would not live long, for I have many enemies".

That Menander did meet a violent end yet remained highly esteemed by his Buddhist subjects is confirmed by Plutarch:

"When Menander, who had ruled with moderation, met his death during an expedition, the villages celebrated his funeral ceremony jointly; they put forth rival claims over his relics, and it was with difficulty that they came to the agreement that each city would receive an equal part of the ashes, and that each of them would have reliquaries of that king".
The learned Plutarch would have been unaware that such funerary honours were reserved by Buddhists for Buddhas and Universal Monarchs (*Chakravartin*) alone».[121]

---

[120]*Ibidem*.
[121]Stephen Batchelor, *The awakening of the West. The encounter of Buddhism and Western culture*, HarperCollins, London, 1994, pp. 13-14.

After Menander I passed away, the territories, the territories on which he had, probably in an enlightened way, governed gradually returned to India and its composite culture.

Many Greeks, remaining in that area of the once-Hellenistic world, converted to Buddhism, leaving the last trace of Hellenism in India and Asia: "the anthropomorphic representation of the Buddha".

In the first five hundred years of Buddhist history, in fact, the Buddha was depicted through only symbols: "an eight-spoked wheel, an empty throne, a teee, a pair of footprints".

The symbolism was not sufficient for the Greek Buddhists of Gandhāra (area of today northern Pakistan and Afghanistan). Thus they portrayed the Buddha with the features of the Greek god Apollo, "who, as a youthful warrior, represents the ideal human form, while also standing for the virtues of healing, purity, moderation and self-knowledge"[122].

«Thus the Greeks, who cavorted into India with Dionysos, crossed the Indus under Alexander, stimulated the birth of the Mauryan dynasty of Chandragupta and Ashoka, penetrated the Gangetic civilization under Demetrius, and established a Graeco-Buddhist culture through Menander, evaporated after a thousand years having bequeathed the image of Apollo»[123].

The art of Gandhāra (of which we have a rich collection of pieces in Rome's National Museum of Oriental Art Giuseppe Tucci) is therefore a very interesting expression of the profound encounter, until the fusion, of the Greek West and Buddhist India.

Because of that encounter, how many traders, soldiers, slaves and also, as writes Amartya Sen, intellectuals, philo-

---

[122]*Ivi*, p. 15.
[123]*Ibidem*.

sophers, reaserchers and Buddhist missionaries of the King Aśoka travelled along the Silk Route?

Therefore, in the time of Jesus, India and the West were not so alien to each other, as we could be tempted to presume. The communications were open and it is at least likely to claim that along with those religions travelled even the founder of Christianity

Considering now the possible permanence of Jesus in India during his youth, or else the hypothesis proposed by Nicholas Notovitch, as it has been already reported the most important documents are the manuscripts found by the Russian traveller (which have disappeared) and the *Natha Namavali Sutra* of the *Nath* sect.

I think it is also useful to remember Swami Abhedananda's journey in Ladakh has been successful.

Indeed the Swami had access to Hemis' manuscripts of which he had translated some fragments.

However, after him, no one else had the chance to consult and translate them.

Then Notovitch's hypothesis is suggestive and had a good response but it is nowadays difficult to corroborate from a scientific point of view.

As I've already written, Hemis' manuscripts should have been deeply analysed, as the Dead Sea and Nag Hammadi scrolls, by scientific *équipes*.

In this way it could have been easier to exclude (or to validate) the hypothesis they were fake and created for disparate purposes.

Considering now the oral sources documented by Nicholas Roerich, I think they can probably help to corroborate the hypothesis Jesus lived in India even if it is still, clearly, a disputable affirmation.

From a methodological point of view, oral sources have a value in the social sciences; in the qualitative sociology and, above all, in the cultural anthropology.

In general I think deeper researches should be done and the hypothesis of Jesus' stay in India during his youth should be investigated even (and, maybe, mostly) at the academic level, comparing the books of Notovitch and Roerich with a fieldwork, collecting tales and popular legends and digging in the libraries of Ladakhi and Himalayan monasteries, looking for other written records and interviewing monks and abbots.

I think it is reasonable to claim at the moment the Notovitch's hypothesis is suggestive but "abstract" although, of course, it is possible to trust it "by faith", with the support of the logic and the plausibility.

I think it is, instead, more structured the Ahmadiyya perspective.

Many scholars have followed the pioneering studies of Mirza Ghulām Ahmad.

The Ahmadiyya, in their Headquarters of Qadian and London, have their own TV, publishing house and team of scholars who continue to do research on the subject in analysis, even publishing monthly an excellent *Review of religions* (www.reviewofreligions.org).

To corroborate their "swoon theory", of Jesus' survival to crucifixion and his death, at an old age, in Kashmir, the Ahmadiyya and the scholars who are following the researches of Mirza Ghulām Ahmad report different documentary sources. We are going to consider some of them, premising that a supporter of both the thesis of Nicholas Notovitch and Mirza Ghulām Ahmad was the Professor Maria Fida Hassnain.

Again about the Jewish origin of Afghan and Kashmiri peoples

Amartya Sen, in *Argumentative India*, one of his most appreciated books has considered the issue in analysis:

«Jews came to India, it appears, shortly after the fall of Jerusalem [at the beginning of the Christian era], though there are other theories as well (including the claim that members of the Bene Israeli community first arrived in the eighth century BCE and, more plausibly, that they came in 175 BCE)»[124].

I think it is useful to remind to the reader that in the eight century BCE the Jews suffered a very tough Assyrian occupation which can be easily considered a good reason, for them, to migrate.

Also the period between 175 and 164 BCE has not been easy for the Jews because they were under the yoke of Hellenistic reign of Antiochus IV Epifanes, notorious for its hardness.

Then Amartya Sen does not exclude ancient Jewish migrations to India and it is more than reasonable to hypothesize the settlement of refugees of the ten, lost, tribes of Israel in the north-western areas of Indian world including the territories of present-day Afghanistan and Kashmir.

I think it is also interesting to report that according to the scholar Aziz Kashmiri, author of *Christ in Kashmir* (mentioned in the Bibliography) the name Kashmir derives from *kasher* (Serrano was claiming the same origin of the name of north-western Indian state).

The meaning of the word *kasher* or *kosher* is "fit for use or consumption, in accordance with Jewish law (especially relating to food)", largely equivalent to the Arabic term *halal*.

---

[124] Amartya Sen, *Argumentative India*, Penguin Books, London, 2006, p. 17.

Considering now the book of Maria Fida Hassnain, *The fifth Gospel* (in my opinion it is one of his best), some Afghan tribes would refer their genealogies to Jewish prophets, others would claim to descend from the Jewish Kish tribe.

Both Assyria and Persia colonised territories of today Afghanistan, writes Hassnain, where they deported people, from present-day Syria, of Jewish ethnicity. For this reason some Afghan tribes still qualify themselves as *Bani-Israel*: Sons of Israel.

Following the Arab occupation, these tribes converted to Islam.

Writes Hassnain:

«Some of the Israeli prophets are buried at Balkh and Ibn-i-Betuta, the famous world traveler, makes special mention about the Tomb of Ezekiel there. Another prophet of the Jews, Samuel, is buried on the side of the road leading to Khurasan from Hamadan. Another Israeli Prophet is buried at Rang–barang near Bajoor in Afghanistan.

It is interesting to note that the Afghans carry their tribal names even at present and use them as cognomen. Prominent among these tribes are the clans of Ammon-zye, Amma-zye, Davood-zye, Abrahim-zye, Shemoo-zye, Yusuf-zye, Ayub-khel, Haroon-khel, Issa-khel, Ishaq-khel, Mysa-khel, Sulaiman-khel, Yayah-khel, Yaqoob-khel, Yunus-khel and Zakaria-khel.

All these clans do possess their ancestral line right up to Jacob.

These records of Rights are also preserved in the Revenue Archives of each region of Afghanistan, Chitral and Peshawar»[125].

Names of Jewish origin and which, in some cases, recall some "local equivalents" of the name of Jesus are also present in Kashmir where, writes Hassnain, was even found an ancient copy of the Torah, in Hebrew, on sheepskin.

---

[125] Maria Fida Hassnain, *The fifth gospel*, Destgir Publications, Srinagar (Kashmir-India), 1988, p. 22

For instance: Aish Muqam, a shrine where are buried some Muslim saints, built on a cave that was an important place of hermitage and asceticism, not far from Srinagar.

«The name *Aish-Muqam* is said to refer to Jesus. *Aish* is said to derive from Isha or Issa and *muqam* means "place of rest (or repose)". This rather suggests that the isolated cave might once have served as a place where Jesus could withdraw for a while to devote himself to quiet meditation. There is, of course, no longer anything to prove the truth of such traditions»[126]

In Aish Muqam is also jealously preserved an ancient rod with magical powers (used in fact in cases of natural disasters) which, in local folklore, is said to have belonged first to Moses, then to Jesus.

Again in relation to possible Jews origin of Afghan people a mention is due to the documentary of Isareli-Canadian film director Simcha Jacobovici *Quest for the lost tribes* (easily available on YouTube).

It is an accurate search, developing through a fascinating journey in different countries of central and southern Asia, of people supposed to be members of the ten lost tribes of Israel[127].

In his filmed journey, Simcha Jacobovici cannot neglect Afghanistan (mostly the area around the Khyber Pass, on the border with Pakistan, home to Pashtun people), looking for the descendents of Zevulun tribe and of Bani Israel.

More precisely, his explicit purpose is to investigate whether, under an Islamic surface, it could be found an Israelite past.

An interesting element Simcha Jacobovici considers is the *Pakhtunwali* (or *Pashtunwali*): a non-written tribal ethical code

---

[126] Holger Kersten, *Jesus lived in India*, Penguin, New Delhi, 2001, p. 262.
[127] These are the tribes of Reuben, Simeon, Dan, Naphtali, Gad, Asher, Issachar, Zebulun, Manasseh, and Ephraim.

and traditional lifestyle followed by the indigenous Pashtun people and based on the "ultimate loyalty".

«Pakhtunwali», affirms Simcha Jacobovici in his documentary, «is Old Testament law in a kind of unforgiving way where you have no kind of rabbinical softening of it. Eye for an eye means eye for an eye, literally».

As in the Bible the Pathans or Pashtuns practice animal sacrifices for religious purposes and some of them light oil lamps on Friday nights to ask for forgiveness and blessing from God.

It is even interesting to mention that the Pathans still live in tribal groups with names recalling Israelite tribes' ones.

For example, the Afghan tribe of Rabbani is recalling the one of Reuben, Levani the one of Levi, Shinwari the one of Simeon and Gadun the one of Gad.

Of course, further research should be done on this topic.

In conclusion of this paragraph I think it is useful to mention an article on *The Guardian* of January 2010: *Pashtun clue to lost tribes of Israel*.

The author, Rory McCarthy, is a postdoctoral fellow at Magdalen College, Oxford, where he works on social movements, contentious politics, and Islamism in the Middle East and North Africa.

The article stated that «Historical and anecdotal evidence strongly suggests a connection, but definitive scientific proof has never been found. Some leading Israeli anthropologists believe that, of all the many groups in the world which claim to have a connection to the 10 lost tribes, the Pashtuns, or Pathans, have the most compelling case».

Jesus' journey into Kashmir

In *Jesus lived in India* Holger Kersten writes "there is evidence for the presence of Jesus in Kashmir that is much more solid than mere oral traditions", as the one, we have just mentioned, of Aish Muqam.

For instance: "testimonies in stone which have survived the vicissitudes of the centuries, more or less intact, as archaeological treasures".

Kersten:

«One such lapidary piece of testimony to the presence of Jesus in Kashmir is an inscription on the *Takht-i-Suleiman*, the "Throne of Solomon", the history of which is recounted by Mullah Nadiri, a historian who lived during the rule of Sultan Zainul Abidin. In his *History of Kashmir* (*Tarikh-i-Kashmir*), written in 1413, he reports that the Temple of Solomon (which was already a thousand years old at the dawn of the Christian era) was restored by a Persian architect, by royal command during the reign of Gopadatta, son of Rajah Akh.
[...]
During the renovation work, four sayings in Old Persian were inscribed at the side of the steps leading up to the grand entrance:

Maimar een satoon raj bihishti zargar, sal panjah wa chahar
"The constructor of these columns is the most humble Bihishti Zargar, in the year fifty and four".

Een satoon bardast khwaja rukun bin murjan
"Khwaja Rukun, son of Murjan, had these columns built".

Dar een wagat yuz asaf dawa-i-paighambar-imikunad. Sal panjah wa chahar
"At this time, Yuz Asaf announced his prophetic mission. In the year fifty and four".

Aishan yuzu paighambar-i-bani israil ast.
"He is Jesus, prophet of the sons of Israel"»[129].

In the following lines Kersten reports a commentary done by Mullah Nadiri:

«At the time of Gopadatta's reign, Yuz Asaf came from the Holy Land up into this valley, and announced that he was a prophet. He epitomised the peak of piety and of virtue, and proclaimed that he was himself his own message, that he lived in God day and night, and that he had made God accessible to the people of Kashmir. He called the people unto him, and the people of the valley believed in him. When the Hindus came to Gopadatta in indignation, pressing him to deal with the man, he turned them away.
I've also read in a Hindu book that this prophet is really Hazrat Issa, the Spirit of God (God's peace and goodwill be on him), and he adopted the name of Yuz Asaf[130]. True knowledge is with God. He spent his life in this valley.
After his passing, his body was laid to rest in Mohalla Anzimarah. It i salso said that the light of prophecy emanates from the tomb of this prophet.
King Gopadatta ruled sixty years and two months, before passing away. After him, his son Gikaran mounted the throne and ruled for the span of fifty eight years»[131]...

Kersten writes Mullah Nadiri's book is not the only one to report Jesus' stay in Kashmir, mentioning (without giving other details) twenty first other references.

---

[129]Holger Kersten, *Jesus lived in India*, op. cit., p. 263.
[130]According to the supporter of the thesis Jesus spent long time in Kashmir after he survived the crucifixion the name Yuz Asaf means: "Leader of the healed". It can be easily related to miraculous healings that made Jesus famous not only in Palestine and, eventually, in India but even in several places he would have crossed in this journey to the East.
[131]Holger Kersten, *Jesus lived in India*, op. cit., pp. 263-264.

He then provides a list of names of cities and Kashmiri places recalling those of Jesus.

They are twenty four, the first is the already mentioned Aish Muqam, I don't report the others to avoid duplication (of course for more information I invite the readers to check Holger Kersten's book *Jesus lived in India*).

As I've written more than one time, the main purpose of Jesus' journey to the East was to prech to Israel's lost tribes who were not just in the north-west part of India (mostly coinciding with present state of Kashmir).

For this reason, as Kersten did analyze in his book, Jesus didn't reach soon Kashmir and his journey — with many, sometimes long, stops — would have lasted about sixteen years.

It is useful to repeat Burke's book *Among the dervishes* presents interesting proofs of a possible Jesus' stay in Afghanistan, on his way to Kashmir.

Shortly considering other testimonies of his journey, Kersten quotes the *Actae Thomae*, where it is mentioned the participation of Jesus, as well as his "skeptic disciple" — who it is today commonly accepted lived long time in India where he died and where he's buried — to the wedding of the daughter of King of Andrapa, in North Anatolia.

«On the same wedding night», writes Kersten, «the King of Andrapa showed the apostle Thomas into the bridal chamber, so that he might convert the newly wedded couple. After Thomas has prayed with the couple, everyone else left the room»[132].

Quoting from *Actae Thomae* (11-12):

«But after everyone had left and the doors had been closed, the bridegroom raised the curtain of the bridal chamber to call his bride. And he saw the Lord Jesus speaking with the bride, re-

---

[132]*Ivi*, p. 245.

sembling Judas Thomas, who had just blessed them and left them. The groom said to Jesus: "Did you not just leave? How did you get back in?" But the Lord replied: I am not Judas surnamed Thomas, I am his brother[133]". And the Lord sat down upon the bed, asking them to sit down on couches, and proceeded to tell them: "Remember, my children, what my brother said to you and to whom he commended you"».

Moving in the direction of Kashmir, another possible proof of his long journey from Palestine is in a small mountain town seventy kilometers east of Taxila: Mari ("anciently written Murree on English topographic maps").

There a tomb known *as Mai Mari da Ashtan* (the resting place of Mother Mary) has been maintained and honored as far back as anyone can remember.

The tomb — located on Pindi Point, a mountain outside the small town — is aligned with east-west orientation, according to Jewish tradition, while in Islamic culture the orientation is north-south.

Today the site, not far from the ceasefire line, is not accessible, belonging to a military exclusion zone.

The alleged tomb of Jesus in Srinagar

I've already writeen about *Rozabal*.

I'm going to add a couple of excerpts from Kersten's book who was able to visit it when it still open to the public.

---

[133] The apostle Thomas was also known as Didymus. This name, as well as the Aramaic Toma, means "twin". It is matter of an interesting debate the possible "brotherhood", allegorical or not, of Thomas and Jesus.

As it has already mentioned in *Rozabal* or Rauza Bal[134] are buried two people: Yuz Asaf (a possible Persina name of Jesus) and the Muslim saint Syed Nasir-Ud-Din.

«Both tomstones are aligned north-south, following Islamic custom. As is also usual for Islamic tombs in India, these tombstones are just markers: the actual graves are located in a crypt below the floor of the building. A tiny opening allows a visitor to look down into the burial chamber below. The sarcophagus containing the earthly remains of Yuz Asaf is aligned east-west, in accordance with Jewish custom! This is clear proof that Yuz Asaf could not have been an Islamic saint. And among the Hindus and Buddhists, only ascetics (*sadhus*) and saints are buried (corpses are normally cremated). So here lies a person who was revered as a saint even before the arrival of Islam, when Kashmir was Mahayana Buddhist and Tantric Hindu.
[...]
Age-old documents state that a protective building had already been constructed over the crypt by AD 112. Since that time, the tomb has been tended by the same family, with the office of tomb attendant being passed down in an unbroken line from father to son. In 1766, the keepers of the tomb were issued with a charter officially confirming the importance of the sacred site. In the formal decree issued by the Grand Mufti (or "Teacher of Islamic religious law") Rahman Mir are the words: "Here lies Yuz Asaf, who rebuilt the Temple of Solomon at the time of King Gopadatta, and who came as a prophet to Kashmir.
He ministered to the people, declared his unity with God, and was a lawgiver to the people. Since then his tomb has been honoured by kings, state officials, high dignitaries and the common folk"»[135].

---

[134]«Rauza is a term used to denote the tomb of a celebrated personality: someone noble, wealthy or saintly». In: Holger Kersten, *Jesus lived in India*, op. cit., p. 271.
[135]Holger Kersten, *Jesus lived in India*, op. cit., pp. 273/276.

Paramahansa Yogananda: the second coming of Jesus

Paramahansa Yogananda is probably the best known Indian 'master' in the West, after Gandhi, Sai Baba and Osho Rajneesh.

I will introduce him starting with the presentation of his *gurus*, quoting the paragraph *Yogic seeds in America* from my book *Yoga based on authentic Indian traditions*.

Sri Yukteswar Giri is the monastic name of Priyanath Karar, born in Serampore, in the Bengali state of India, on the 10th of may 1855. Initiated into the monastic Swami order after the death of his wife, he met, in 1884, Lahiri Mahasaya, a prestigious guru living in Benares, becoming his devotee pupil and getting the initiation to *Kriya Yoga*.

This is an ancient yoga system (connected by Paramahansa Yogananda with the teachings of Krishna who, according to traditional Indian scriptures and astrological calculations, lived between 3228 and 3102 BC) revived in modern times by Mahavatar Babaji through his main disciple, the already mentioned Lahiri Mahasaya.

Spending some more words about Mahavatar Babaji, he's an Indian and quite mysterious saint.

Nobody knows his real name and date of birth.

He has been called Mahavatar Babaji by Lahiri Mahasaya who met him between 1861 and 1935.

"Mahavatar" means "great avatar" (divine incarnation), and "Babaji" simply means "revered father".

Lahiri Mahasaya wrote in his diary that Mahavatar Babaji was the reincarnation of Lord Krishna, traditionally considered an avatar of Vishnu, to whom the authorship of *Bhagavadgīta* is traditionally attributed.

In 1894, while attending the Kumbha Mela in Allahabad, Sri Yukteswar met Mahavatar Babaji who asked him to write a book comparing Hindu scriptures and the Christian Bible.

Sri Yukteswar fulfilled the desire of the great saint writing, in the same year, *Kaivalya Darsanam* or *The Holy Science* which inspired numberless spiritual researchers.

The dialogue between Mahavatar Babaji and Sri Yukteswar, at that Kumbha Mela, was crucial for the events which were to follow and also for the main goal of this book: to contribute to intercultural dialogue between India and the West, for mutual growth.

It is important to introduce this dialogue mentioning the inner feeling of Sri Yukteswar attending the gathering.

He was quite disappointed.

In fact in Kumbha Mela (I attended the event — it is the biggest traditional Hindu gathering organized every three years in one of four Indian holy towns: Haridwar, Nasik, Ujjain and Allahabad — on more than one occasion) it is possible to meet great saints but even — and more often — great scoundrels.

Then, Sri Yukteswar was positively thinking about the more rational western world when he was called by Mahavatar Babaji.

I quote the crucial passages of their dialogue from *Autobiography of a yogi*, a very famous bestseller written by the main pupil of Sri Yukteswar: Paramhansa Yogananda and published in 1946.

Yogananda reports the tale from the mouths of Sri Yukteswar:

«My smouldering reflections on social reform were interrupted by the voice of a tall sannyasi who halted before me.

"Sir", he said, "a saint is calling you".
"Who is he?"
"Come and see for yourself".
Hesitantly following this laconic advice, I soon found myself near a tree whose branches were sheltering a guru with an attractive group of disciples. The master, a bright unusual figure, with sparkling dark eyes, rose at my approach and embraced me.
"Welcome, Swamiji", he said affectionately.
"Sir", I replied emphatically, "I am not a swami".
"Those on whom I am divinely directed to bestow the title of swami never cast it off". The saint addressed me simply, but deep conviction of truth rang in his words; I was engulfed in an instant wave of spiritual blessing. Smiling at my sudden elevation into the ancient monastic order, I bowed at the feet of the obviously great and angelic being in human form who had thus honored me.
Babaji — for it was indeed he — motioned me to a seat near him under the tree. He was strong and young, and looked like Lahiri Mahasaya; yet the resemblance did not strike me, even though I had often heard of the extraordinary similarities in the appearance of the two masters.
Babaji possesses a power by which he can prevent any specific thought from arising in a person's mind.
Evidently the great guru wished me to be perfectly natural in his presence, not overawed by knowledge of his identity.
"What do you think of the Kumbha Mela?".
"I was greatly disappointed, sir", I added hastily, "Up until the time I met you. Somehow saints and this commotion don't seem to belong together".
"Child", the master said, though apparently I was nearly twice his own age, "for the faults of the many, judge not the whole. Everything on earth is of mixed character, like a

mingling of sand and sugar. Be like the wise ant which seizes only the sugar, and leaves the sand untouched.
Though many sadhus here still wander in delusion, yet the Mela is blessed by a few men of God-realization".
In view of my own meeting with this exalted master, I quickly agreed with his observation.
"Sir", I commented, "I have been thinking of the scientific men of the West, greater by far in intelligence than most people congregated here, living in distant Europe and America, professing different creeds, and ignorant of the real values of such Melas as the present one.
They are the men who could benefit greatly by meetings with India's masters. But, although high in intellectual attainments, many Westerners are wedded to rank materialism. Others, famous in science and philosophy, do not recognize the essential unity in religion. Their creeds serve as insurmountable barriers that threaten to separate them from us forever".
"I saw that you are interested in the West, as well as the East". Babaji's face beamed with approval. "I felt the pangs of your heart, broad enough for all men, whether Oriental or Occidental. That is why I summoned you here. East and West must establish a golden middle path of activity and spirituality combined", he continued. "India has much to learn from the West in material development; in return, India can teach the universal methods by which the West will be able to base its religious beliefs on the unshakable foundations of yogic science. You, Swamiji, have a part to play in the coming harmonious exchange between Orient and Occident. Some years hence I shall send you a disciple whom you can train for yoga dissemination in the West"»[136].

---

[136]ParamahansaYogananda, *Autobiography of a yogi*, Original 1946 Edition, pp. 312-313.

Approximately one year before this meaningful dialogue, the fifth of January 1893, in Gorakhpur (Indian town in the northern state of Uttar Pradesh), not far from Lahiri Mahasaya's living place — Benares or Varanasi — born Mukunda Lal Ghosh, later known (in 1915, when he took formal vows into the monastic Swami Order) as Swami Yogananda Giri.

He met Swami Sri Yukteswar Giri in 1910, at the age of 17. Ten years later he was on the ship *City of Sparta* going to the US. He was India's delegate to an International Congress of Religious Liberals convening in Boston.

Following the dialogue between Mahavatar Babaji and Sri Yukteswar, Yogananda was the pupil candidate to disseminate yoga in the West.

In 1920 he even founded, in the U.S., the *Self-Realization Fellowship* (SRF) for that purpose.

He lectured and taught in a number of places in America, attracting thousands of students, including soprano Amelita Galli-Curci, tenor Vladimir Rosing and Clara Clemens Gabrilowitsch, the daughter of Mark Twain.

In 1925 he established an international centre for *Self-Realization Fellowship* in Los Angeles, California, becoming the first Hindu teacher of yoga to make his permanent home in America.

Because of that he is mentioned, with Swami Vivekananda (famous pupil of Bengali saint Ramakrishna), by the writer Dr. Wendell Thomas, in the book *Hinduism invades America* (published in 1930).

This is a meaningful quote from that book:

«I came to Paramahansa Yogananda many years ago, not as a seeker, but as a writer with a sympathetic yet analytic and critical approach. I found in him a rare combination. While steadfast in the ancient principles of his profound faith, he had the gift of generous adaptability, so that he became Christian and American without ceasing to be Hindu and Indian. With his quick wit and great spirit, he was well fitted to promote reconciliation and truth among the religious seekers of the world. He brought peace and joy to multitudes».

A whole chapter of Dr. Wendell's book was dedicated to Yogananda's *Yogoda System* and *Yogoda Satsanga Organization*.

Yogananda went back in India in 1935–1936. He met Mahatma Gandhi (sharing the ideals of passive resistance and nonviolence and conferring to him the initiation to *Kriya Yoga*), the Bengali saint Anandamoyi Ma, Nobel-winning physicist Chandrasekhara Venkata Raman and several disciples of Lahiri Mahasaya.

He got from his guru, Sri Yukteswar, the monastic title of *Paramahansa*: "supreme swan", indicating the highest spiritual attainment.

After his visit to India and his ultimate farewell to his Guru (who passed away in Puri, in the Indian state of Orissa) the 9th of March 1936, he went back to America where he also passed away on the 7th of March 1952[137].

---

[137] Quoting from Wikipedia:

In the days leading up to his death, he began hinting that it was time for him to leave the world. On March 7, 1952, he attended a dinner for the visiting Indian Ambassador to the U.S., Binay Ranjan Sen, and his wife at the Biltmore Hotel in Los Angeles. At the conclusion of the banquet Yogananda spoke of India and America, their contributions to world peace and human progress, and their future cooperation, expressing his hope for a "United World" that would combine the best qualities of "efficient America" and "spiritual India". According to two eyewitnesses — long-time disciples Swami Kriyananda and Daya Mata — as Yogananda ended his speech, he read from his poem *My India*, concluding with the words "Where Ganges, woods, Himalayan caves, and men dream God — I am hallowed; my body touched that sod". At the very last words, he slid to the floor, dead from a heart attack.

Unusually, his body remained uncorrupted for three weeks after his death as witnessed and documented by the director of Forest Lawn Memorial Park Cemetery.

From original *Self-Realization Fellowship* — headquartered in Los Angeles — several meditation centres and temples have been founded across the world.

Even *World Brotherhood Colonies*, intentional communities rooted in simple yogic principles, have been founded by Yogananda's main American pupil: Swami Kriyananda.

There are several in the U.S., one in Italy (near Assisi) and three in India.

Coming now to Yogananda's considerations about the connections between Jesus and India, he emphasises the vivacity of commercial relations between the West and the East since ancient times.

At this regards he quotes the second book of Chronicles.
In particular the following two passages are of interest:

«And the servants also of Huram, and the servants of Solomon, which brought gold from Ophir, brought algum trees and precious stones.
And the king made of the algum trees terraces to the house of the Lord, and to the king's palace, and harps and psalteries for singers: and there were none such seen before in the land of Judah».
(II Chronicles 9:10-11)

Kriyananda wrote that Yogananda had once stated in a lecture, "A heart attack is the easiest way to die. That is how I choose to die".
Yogananda's remains are interred at the Forest Lawn Memorial Park in Glendale, California.

«And all the drinking vessels of king Solomon were of gold, and all the vessels of the house of the forest of Lebanon were of pure gold: none were of silver; it was not anything accounted of in the days of Solomon.
For the king's ships went to Tarshish with the servants of Huram: every three years once came the ships of Tarshish bringing gold, and silver, ivory, and apes, and peacocks».
(II Chronicles 9:20-21)

Ophir, according to what is reported in *The second coming of Christ*, composed by aggregating the contents of several books written by Yogananda, should be located not far from modern day Mumbai.

Yogananda is not the only one identifying Ophir (an unidentified region famous in Old Testament) with an Indian location.

Actually the name of this place appears in other passages of the Old Testament.

In the Book of Kings[138], in the Book of Psalms[139] and in the Book of Isaiah[140].

---

[138]«And king Solomon made a navy of ships in Ezion-geber, which is beside Eloth, on the shore of the Red Sea, in the land of Edom. And Hiram sent in the navy his servants, shipmen that had knowledge of the sea, with the servants of Solomon. And they came to Ophir, and fetched from thence gold, four hundred and twenty talents, and brought it to king Solomon». (I Kings, 9: 26-28)

«And she gave the king a hundred and twenty talents of gold, and of spices very great store, and precious stones; there came no more such abundance of spices as these which the queen of Sheba gave to king Solomon. And the navy also of Hiram, that brought gold from Ophir, brought in from Ophir great plenty of sandal-wood and precious stones».
(I Kings, 10: 10-11)

[139]«All your garments are fragrant with myrrh and aloes and cassia; from palaces of ivory the harps make you glad. The daughters of kings are

However the location of Ophir has been disputed for a long time. Some historian and scholars claimed it was a place in Arabian peninsula or somewhere in Africa, others, such as Flavius Josephus, identified Ophir with *Aurea Chersonesus*, belonging to India but, roughly, corresponding to the Malacca peninsula in the modern world[141].

The Septuagint Bible translated Ophir as Souphir.

The name is reminiscent of Sopara, an ancient port town capital of ancient India's geographical region Aparanta or Aparatanka, on the western coastline of the country.

The place, nowadays named Nala Sopara, at approximately 57 km from Mumbai, has a long and interesting history (the earliest reference occurs in Mahabharata as Shuparak), mostly of trading with Mesopotamia, Egypt, Arabia and Eastern Africa.

The Buddhist text *Mahavamsa* (VI, 46,47) states that Prince Vijaya — the future first, legendary, king of Sri Lanka — sailed from Supparaka (Sopara) to the island that would later become his kingdom.

---

among your honored women; the queen stands at your right hand, adorned with the gold of Ophir». (Psalms, 45: 8-9)

[140]«I will make a man more precious than fine gold; even a man than the golden wedge of Ophir». (Isaiah, 13: 12)

[141]«Moreover the King built many ships in the Egyptian bay of the Red Sea; in a certain place called Ezion-geber. It is now called Berenice; and is not far from the city Eloth. This country belonged formerly to the Jews; and became useful for shipping, from the donations of Hiram King of Tyre. For he sent a sufficient number of men thither for pilots, and such as were skilful in navigation: to whom Solomon gave this command, that they should go along with his own stewards to the land that was of old called Ophir, but now the Aurea Chersonesus, which belongs to India, to fetch him gold. And when they had gathered four hundred talents together, they returned to the King again».
(*Antiquities* 8:6:4)

His reign is traditionally dated to 543–505 BCE.

The relevance of ancient Sopara also for Buddhism is confirmed by the finding of a stupa and fragments of two major rock edicts of Emperor Ashoka[142] — the eighth and ninth ones — in 1882.

As ancient prominent port on the West coast of India, Sopara has been identified by some historians as biblical Ophir/Souphir.

However there are also other interesting hypothesis related to the possible Indian location of ancient Ophir.

Sir William Smith, author in 1863 of *A Dictionary of the Bible*, highlights the nature of imports destined for King Solomon: "gold, silver, ivory, ape and peacocks" (as it is mentioned in II Chronicles 9:20-2), concluding that "the peacocks point conclusively not to Africa but to India"[143].

Then Sir William Smith integrates his affirmation with the following analysis:

«The inference to be drawn from the importation of peacocks is confirmed by the Hebrew names for ape and peacock. Neither of these names is of Hebrew, or even Shemitic origin; and each points to India. Thus the Hebrew word for ape is *kôph*, while the Sanscrit word is *kapi*. Again the Hebrew word for peacock is *tukki*, which cannot be explained in Hebrew, but is akin to *tôka* in the Tamil language, in which it is likewise capable of explanation. It is only to be added, that there are not sufficient data for determining what were the ports in India or the Indian Islands which were reached by the fleet of Hiram and Solomon»[144].

Here Ophir is not considered as a possible Indian location.

---

[142] Emperor Ashoka ruled almost all of the Indian subcontinent from approximately 268 to 232 BCE. He is well presented in the Appendix.
[143] Smith W., *A comprehensive dictionary of the Bible*, D. Appleton and Company, New York, 1871, p. 1089.
[144] *Ibidem*.

According to Sir William Smith it should have been in Arabia while the possible emporium in India could have been Tarshish, mentioned in II Chronicles 9: 20-2.

Sir William Smith even hypothesized the expression "ships of Tarshish" "had come to signify large Phoenician ships, of a particular size and description, destined for long voyages"[145].

The terminological issue has inspired some historians and scholars to identify Ophir as a port in the area known, in ancient times, as Tamilakkam (covering the territories of today Indian states of Tamil Nadu, Kerala and southern parts of Andhra Pradesh and Karnataka), probably corresponding to modern day Poovar in the Thiruvananthapuram District or Beypore, in the Kozhikodeone. Both are in modern day State of Kerala. I think further research should be done on this matter. The ancient relation between India and Middle East certainly has its relevance for the topic of this book.

Great emphasis is also given by Paramahansa Yogananda to the visit of three wise men to the cradle of Jesus.

In his opinion they were coming from India (he does not provide strong historical evidences for this view, and it could form another area of further research, possibly with Yogananda's pupils) to corroborate the future "divine mission" of the unborn child. A mission that, according to Yogananda, had its source in the East.

When Jesus grew up — in the years of his life not reported in the Gospels — he reciprocated their visit to honour the link he had with the *rishis* (seers) of India.

---

[145]*Ibidem.*

Then the teachings of Jesus, even having, according to Yogananda, a Divine origin, would have been also the result of his sapiential studies, which for the most part took place in the East.

This hypothesis, claims Yogananda, is in tune with the universality of the Christ consciousness, which knows no boundaries of race or creed. Even the birthplace of Jesus, Palestine, again according to Yogananda, was not accidental, being in a strategic geographical position. Indeed Palestine could be considered as a crucial western outpost of the Silk Road and other caravan routes that linked India and China to the Mediterranean world (therefore to the Egypt, Greece and Rome) and then, to use the definition of Yogananda: one "divine liaison to unite God-loving peoples of East and West"[146]. For this reason, concludes Yogananda, what he has received from his gurus and the revered masters of India is also found in the teachings of Jesus Christ.

The same teachings, considered in their most authentic and universal expression, are a kind of corner stone to realise a virtuous synthesis of Indian and European cultures and, through mutual compensation, they can be a compass to follow the "golden middle path" pointed out by Mahavatar Babaji.

---

[146]ParamahansaYogananda, *The second coming of Christ* (Vol. I), YogodaSatsanga Society of India, 2007, p. 89.

The Shroud of Turin – The Burial Cloth of Jesus?

This chapter has been authored by Mr Arif Ahmed Khan, Deputy Editor – Christian Section of The Review of Religions *Magazine of the Ahmadiyya Muslim Community.*
The views expressed in this publication are not necessarily the belief of the Ahmadiyya Muslim Community.

The four people in this photo were all brought together, from different continents of the world, in an unusual series of the events.

This photo was taken on July 30th 2017 at the completion of a very unique event that took place deep in the Hampshire countryside, in the South of England.

The event was the first International Shroud of Turin Conference organised by *The Review of Religions* magazine.
Over the course of three days, talks were given by leading experts from around the world and thousands of visitors

were able to view a unique exhibition and replica of the famous cloth.

Moving from left to right on the photograph: Bruno Barberis had travelled from Turin; Barrie Schwortz from Colorado; Arif Khan from London and Manuel Olivares who lives and works between London and India.

What had brought them together?

A single, enigmatic Christian relic.; the Shroud of Turin, a piece of linen alleged to be the actual burial cloth of Jesus Christ [peace be upon him] and preserved for over 2000 years.

The conference took place at the annual gathering of the *Ahmadiyya Muslim Community* in the UK. In 2018 and 2019 additional researchers and experts have attended along with Schwortz, including Emanuela Marinelli from Italy, David Rolfe from England, and Cambridge University lecturer, Dr Peter Wadhams.

For Barrie, 2019 was the 5th consecutive year he had attended the gathering to talk about the Shroud of Turin.

Why would Barrie, a Jewish man, come to a Muslim community to talk about a Christian relic?

The answer to this lies deep within one of the most studied objects in human history.

There are many relics relating to Jesus Christ [peace be upon him], yet this piece of cloth exhibits something quite unique; a detailed image of a crucified man which — to this day — no scientist has been able to fully explain or reproduce.

What Exactly is the Shroud of Turin?

The Shroud of Turin is the alleged burial cloth of Jesus Christ [peace be upon him]. The cloth measures 4.37m by 1.1m and exhibits a faint image of what would appear to be a crucified man. This famous cloth has attracted millions of visitors during exhibitions of the Shroud that take place periodically (the most recent in 2015).

The Shroud is a fascinating cloth that divides opinions. Is it the true burial cloth of Jesus Christ, proving a miraculous Resurrection, or a medieval fake exposed by modern day science?

The Gospels in the New Testament do in fact state that after the Crucifixion, Jesus Christ ^(peace be upon him) was wrapped in a linen cloth:

«And he bought fine linen, and took him down, and wrapped him in the linen, and laid him in a sepulchre which was hewn out of a rock, and rolled a stone unto the door of the sepulchre».

(Mark 15:46)

«And there came also Nicodemus, which at the first came to Jesus by night, and brought a mixture of myrrh and aloes, about a hundred pound [weight]. Then took they the body of Jesus, and wound it in linen clothes with the spices, as the manner of the Jews is to bury».

(John 19:39-40)

The proponents of the Shroud of Turin believe it to be this very same burial cloth used to wrap the body of Jesus after he was taken down from the cross. There have been other claims made with respect to this heritage, but the Shroud of Turin is accepted as the most impressive and most plausible.

What links the Shroud to Jesus and the Crucifixion?

There are a number of significant details on the cloth that seem to correlate with what the Gospels narrate happened to Jesus [peace be upon him] on the cross almost 2000 years ago.

Flagrum & Whipping

It was a common Roman practice to beat and flog the prisoner before Crucifixion.

The Shroud clearly shows such marks, particularly on the back of the body. The Roman instrument used at the time was a whip with three prongs; the tips of these prongs contained bone, shaped to inflict maximum damage and to tear at the flesh.

On the Shroud we see scores of these marks consistent with the Roman torture instrument, the Flagrum[158].

Crown of Thorns

One distinctive feature of Jesus' Crucifixion is that he was mocked for claiming to be the King of the Jews.

In the Gospel account by Matthew, Mark and John we find mention of a 'crown of thorns'.

«And when they had platted a crown of thorns, they put [it] upon his head, and a reed in his right hand: and they bowed the knee before him, and mocked him, saying, Hail, King of the Jews!»

(Matthew 27:29)

---

[158] Ian Wilson & Barrie Schwortz, *The Turin Shroud: The Illustrated Evidence*, 2000, pp. 57.

«And they clothed him with purple, and platted a crown of thorns, and put it about his [head]»

(Mark 15:17)

«And the soldiers platted a crown of thorns, and put [it] on his head, and they put on him a purple robe»

(John 19:2)

The Shroud of Turin shows unusual blood flows around the top of the head and traces of blood in the hair and especially the back of the head. All these are consistent with what we would have expected if a crown of thorns was worn[159].

Nail Wounds

Jesus [peace be upon him] would most likely have been nailed to the cross with nails driven through the wrists and feet. Again, the Shroud depicts just this, with large noticeable blood flows present in both these areas of the cloth.

The nails in the hands are particularly interesting, as traditional depictions suggest the nails went through the palms.

Modern research has shown this would not be possible, and to support the weight of the body the nails would have to have been through the wrists[160].

The evidence in the Shroud is consistent with modern understanding.

---

[159] Ian Wilson & Barrie Schwortz, *The Turin Shroud: The Illustrated Evidence*, 2000, pp. 57-58.
[160] *Ivi*, pp. 58-59.

Blood Flows

As mentioned already, there is blood to be found on the cloth.

In 1978, scientists were quickly able to prove this was real blood from a human and not paint, pigment or animal blood. Also, the blood flows are anatomically correct.

Each of the flows traces the correct lines based upon human anatomy and the arrangement of vessels and arteries[161].

The Unique Image on the Shroud

There is one aspect of the Shroud of Turin that makes it stand out from all other religious artefacts; the presence of a unique image. This status of the Shroud of Turin was confirmed when, in 1898, the first photograph was taken of the Shroud by Secondo Pia.

The negative produced from this photograph revealed amazing levels of detail in the Shroud.

Instead of the faint image that had been seen so far, the negative revealed a detailed image.

Secondo Pia reportedly almost dropped the plate due to the shock he felt when he first viewed the photographic plate.

The next major discovery relating to characteristics of the image on the Shroud was unlocked with the help of an imaging technology system called a VP-8.

This device was able to analyse the different levels of darkness of the image on the cloth.

There was a theory that the image contained depth information; meaning that the closer a feature of the body was to the cloth the darker that part of the image.

---

[161] *Ivi*, p. 60.

In 1976, scientists at Sandia Laboratories applied this technique to a photograph of the Shroud and witnessed the remarkable output.

The output showed an accurate image with the correct parts of a human face elevated.

This fascinated the two scientists present (Dr Eric Jumper and Dr John Jackson) and they decided to form a research team to investigate what could possibly cause an image like to form on the cloth. This was the birth of STURP, the **Shroud of Turin Research Project**.

STURP – Detailed Scientific Examination of the Shroud in 1978

In 1978, the STURP team conducted a series of non-destructive tests on the Shroud. This team was formed of 33 of the leading scientists and experts in their field, assembled purely to study the Shroud of Turin in detail over a 5-day period. Barrie Schwortz, pictured earlier, was the official documenting photographer for the team. To this day he continues to share his knowledge and experience of examining the Shroud first hand in 1978. He set up the website — *www.shroud.com* — in 1996 and it is the primary online source for information about the Shroud.

The data collected from those detailed scientific tests done in 1978, almost 40 years later, still forms the main source of empirical data relating to the Shroud. No other scientific examinations have taken place since 1978.

The focus of their experiments was to understand how the image was formed. STURP concluded that there are certain features of the image on the Shroud that make it difficult to suggest a mechanism that would account for all these features. Any theory about how the image formed must account for all the following characteristics:

1. The image is extremely faint, appearing only on the very upper fibres of the cloth.
2. There is no pigment or dyes contained in the image areas.
3. The further the body is from the cloth, the more faint the image – this leads to what is known as the '3D' quality of the Shroud.
4. The image is a negative.

Despite an intensive period of testing, this question remains unanswered to this day. Another detailed examinationsimilar to the one carried out by STURP has never taken place, leaving this deep mystery unresolved.

How old is the Turin Shroud?

Dating the Shroud of Turin has become a highly controversial area.

To obtain some confirmation of its claims of being from the 1st Century, a carbon dating experiment was planned and the required permissionsobtained.

The method of carbon dating had been used to date famous archaeological artefacts, such as the Dead Sea Scrolls, in the past.

The Shroud made international headlines in 1988 when carbon dating tests carried out by four independent laboratories dated the Shroud to 1260 – 1360 CE. This seemed to settle the issue of whether the cloth was a fake or not. It also fitted the known history of the Shroud, as no confirmed record existed of this Shroud before this period.

The scientists were particularly dismissive of the Shroud and heralded this as some sort of triumph of science over religion.

The following account is taken from the obituary of Professor Edward Hall and summarises the views of others on the Shroud when the carbon dating results were announced:

«There was a multi-million-pound business in making forgeries during the 14th century," he bluntly told a British Museum press conference. "Someone just got a bit of linen, faked it up and flogged it." And again, "Some people may continue to fight for the authenticity of the shroud, like the Flat Earth Society, but this settles it all as far as we are concerned».[162]

The Carbon Dating Result: More Questions than Answers

For scholars and experts, however, the carbon dating result leads to more questions than answers. If this had been 'faked' how was the image produced? How was a 'negative' image created deliberately before the science of photography was understood? How were the anatomically correct blood flows marked when there was incomplete knowledge of anatomy at the time the cloth was supposed to have been created?

The carbon dating result also went against research that was being published by prominent researchers and historians about a possible history of the Shroud that extended far beyond the medieval times. It is true that the recorded history of the Shroud of Turin only dates back to the 13th / 14th century, yet recorded history of a cloth bearing the

---

[162] https://www.independent.co.uk/news/obituaries/professor-edward-hall-9260740.html

image of Jesus Christ ^(peace be upon him) dates back almost two thousand years.

Cloth of Edessa

Historian and Shroud researcher Ian Wilson details a possible timeline for the Shroud dating back to the 1st Century[163]. Wilson draws on research and recorded traditions that talk about a famous cloth bearing the face or imprint of Jesus' face. This cloth is known as the cloth of Edessa[164]. 3rd and 4th Century sources recount the tradition that a cloth 'imprinted with Jesus' likeness'[165] was taken from Jerusalem to Edessa, which was instrumental in converting Edessa's King Abgar V to Christianity. Wilson shows how the cloth appeared to have survived through the centuries and paints a plausible picture of how the Turin Shroud really is the same cloth as the cloth of Edessa and thus centuries old.

If the cloth of Edessa is the same cloth as the Shroud of Turin, then the date given by the carbon dating results cannot be correct. Could the carbon dating result be wrong and, if so, what could account for such a large discrepancy between the expected date and the result the tests returned?

Scholars looked for things that could point to an inaccuracy in the carbon dating results. Reputable scholars put out theories about the error in carbon dating, talked of a 'bio-plastic' coating, and also speculation about how fire damage could have affected the result. There were also conspiracy theories, talking of scientists and Vatican officials conspiring to skew the dating results. However, no suitable explanation was given and for many the 'case had been closed' in terms

---

[163] Turin Shroud: The New Evidence – Discovery HD, April 2009.
[164] *Ibidem.*
[165] *Ibidem.*

of the Shroud of Turin having any chance of being the original burial cloth of Jesus Christ ^(peace be upon him). This remained the case until 2005.

Ray Rogers – Turning the Carbon Dating Result on its Head

In 2005, this mystery appeared to have been solved by Raymond Rogers, an expert in thermodynamics and one of the original members of the STURP team.
The research by Rogers centred around a theory proposed by a husband and wife team, Sue Benford and Joseph Marino. It should be understood that Benford and Marino are not scientists and their theory was based upon analysis of existing images of the Shroud from 1978.

What the couple observed was that the section of the cloth from which the radio carbon sample was taken looked to have been rewoven. Barrie Schwortz talked about this in a documentary on the Shroud:

«They had taken photographs that were available of the samples used for the carbon dating and they had submitted these to several textiles experts who did not know they were looking at photos of the Shroud. Each of these textiles experts, independent of each other said, 'You know, this looks rewoven».[166]

Benford and Marino believed that the section was repaired using 16th century cotton. The original cloth and the 16th century cotton cloth would be mixed and interwoven.

---

[166] *Ibidem.*

Benford and Marino argued that this mixture of the original 1st century cloth, along with 16th century cotton would lead to a carbon dating result in between the two dates.

They published this in a paper entitled "Evidence for the Skewing of the C-14 Dating of the Shroud of Turin Due to Repairs". It was this paper that grabbed the attention of Ray Rogers. Rogers described in an interview his motivations for the work:

«I had given up on the Shroud and this is about the same time that the lunatic fringe were coming up with an infinite number of ways in which the date could be wrong, and this [paper by Benford and Marino] was just the last straw».

Barrie Schwortz explains how he got a call from Ray Rogers about the paper:

«I got a call from Ray and he's like 'what the hell is this? This is nonsense, I can prove these people wrong in 5 minutes; I said 'Well, Ray, go for it'».

Ray was in a unique position to investigate this theory as he had in his possession samples from both the radiocarbon sample area of the Shroud as well as a sample from an adjacent section to the radiocarbon sample area.

Barrie Schwortz explains how hours after setting out to prove this theory wrong Rogers called him again:

«He calls me a couple of hours later and he says 'Boy, you know, they were right. There is cotton here! There is no cotton in the rest of the Shroud. There is cotton interwoven here; they must be right'».

Carbon Dating Sample Invalid

He concluded that the theory was right in stating that the section of the cloth used for the carbon dating was actually a rewoven section.

Sadly, Raymond Rogers lost his battle with cancer shortly after completing this work. His entire testimony on this research was documented by Shroud expert and colleague, Barrie Schwortz, and then published as a DVD. Just weeks before Ray passed away, a detailed article containing his findings was published in the peer reviewed Chemistry journal "ThermochimicaActa"[167].

This was revolutionary for the research. Now the carbon dating result was declared invalid and the biggest objection to the Shroud's possible authenticity removed. Or was it?

To this day, the significance of Ray Rogers' work seems not to have permeated anywhere near as far as the carbon dating news. Outside expert circles, few are aware of or talk about this work by Ray Rogers. The carbon dating of the Shroud, however, is far more extensively talked about and known about.

What Does the Shroud Show – Did Jesus Survive the Crucifixion?

The Shroud of Turin is, therefore, a relic that brings with it more debate and split opinions than any other.

It is also allegedly the most studied artefact in human history, with literally thousands of papers and hundreds of books written about it.

---

[167] Studies on the radiocarbon sample from the Shroud of Turin, ThermochimicaActa, Volume 425, Issues 1-2, pp.189

As if this was not controversial enough, there is one more aspect to consider; could the Shroud of Turin help shed light on the Resurrection of Jesus from the dead, a cornerstone of the Christian faith?

For Ahmadi Muslims like me, who believe in Jesus Christ (peace be upon him) having survived the Crucifixion, the Shroud of Turin is a possible piece of evidence to support this view.

There are those who have concluded, from studying the Shroud, that Jesus (peace be upon him) did survive the Crucifixion.

There is an absence of any sign of decomposition of the body, the even nature of the image, the large volume of blood on the cloth and the fact an image formed at all.

Below are two examples of authors who are proponents of the view that the Shroud covered a living body that was in a state of near-death:

Rodney Hoare – The Turin Shroud is Genuine – 1994

Hoare writes about taking images from the Shroud to a group of forensic scientists belonging to the FBI. He writes about the discussions they had based upon the cloth and their arriving at the following conclusion:

«The forensic scientists argued that the body in the Shroud was absolutely dead by pre-seventeenth century standards but in a deep coma by present-day one».[168]

He explains the reasoning for this:

«Any chemical staining reaction…would almost certainly have depended on temperature: the higher the temperature the darker the stain…so the temperature of the cloth must also have been

---

[168] Rodney Hoare, *The Turin Shroud is Genuine*, 1994, p 69.3

approximately uniform. This could only happen if the blood were still circulating, the heart just beating....The body must have been in a coma, therefore, and not clinically dead by twentieth-century standards».[169]

Hoare presents his evidence from the Shroud along with details about the Crucifixion from the New Testament to argue that Jesus survived the Crucifixion.

Holger Kersten &Elmar Gruber – The Jesus Conspiracy – 1992

The central premise of *The Jesus Conspiracy*, by Kersten and Gruber, is that Jesus [peace be upon him] survived the Crucifixion. One of the later sections of their text is entitled 'The Image of a Living Person' and starts as follows:

«After all that we have described there can be no doubt: the Turin cloth is the cloth in which Jesus was placed for healing after being taken down from the Cross. If this is so and Jesus really was still alive when he was placed in the tomb, we should be able to find evidence of the fact on the Turin cloth»[170]

The authors of *The Jesus Conspiracy* draw our attention to the blood marks in particular when arguing their case. The quantity of blood, the flows of blood and experiments they performed themselves all lead Kersten and Gruber to conclude that Jesus was wrapped in the Shroud and he was still alive at the time.

---

[169] *Ivi*, pp.68-69.
[170] Holger Kersten &Elmar Gruber, *The Jesus Conspiracy*, 1992, p.281.

Dead or Alive?

It is a highly controversial area and it is not helped by sensationalised approaches to discussions on the theory that the Shroud shows Jesus ^(peace be upon him) survived.

Conspiracy theories, such as that outlined by Holger Kersten in his book, *The Jesus Conspiracy*, have made it easier for researchers to dismiss the thesis that the Shroud proves Jesus ^(peace be upon him) survived the Crucifixion. On the other side, the biggest proponent of the view that it proves Jesus ^(peace be upon him) died is Dr Frederick Zugibe who is a committed Christian.

More research is required and more questions need answering.

Currently, it seems the evidence available is inconclusive.

People have argued for both outcomes using the same empirical evidence.

Conclusion

It is very difficult to have objective research carried out on the Shroud of Turin, as almost all those interested in the cloth, and involved in the research, have pre-existing biases and beliefs.

Barrie Schwortz's impartiality, given his Jewish origin, is one major blessing for the world of Shroud research. His commitment to objectivity, and the scientific method, have been essential for maintaining balance around such an emotive topic.

Current scholarly opinion is still divided on the Shroud.

Many lost interest after the initial carbon dating result appeared to show it was a fake and a middle age forgery; many are still unaware of Ray Roger's work and findings.

Even as recently as October 2009, there have been researchers claiming to have reproduced the image exposing it as a fake[171].

Some Shroud researchers and enthusiasts want another Carbon-14 dating test to be performed on the Shroud of Turin but access to the cloth is closely controlled and obtaining permission for more tests has historically proven extremely difficult.

In the last decade, it has been noticed that the faint image had started to fade and disappear.

The Shroud was moved to a specially designed container to help preserve it and avoid the image being lost. As part of this process it was treated with Thymol and experts have said this could badly affect any future attempts to date the cloth using C-14.

For the scientists and academics, the Shroud poses a wonderful puzzle to which a solution is still elusive.

For believers in Jesus (peace be upon him) it provides a visual representation of the ordeal of the Crucifixion and the suffering he would have undergone.

For those who support the idea that Jesus (peace be upon him) survived the Crucifixion, it could yet prove to be one of the strongest pieces of evidence available to prove this thesis.

For now, however, there is much debate about all areas of the Shroud. Time will tell if a consensus can ever be reached on the cloth.

---

[171] Italian researcher Professsor Luigi Garlaschelli claimed to have reproduced the Shroud image using medieval techniques on October 6th 2009. Experts quickly pointed out the theory put forward by the Professor had already been examined previously and ruled out on several accounts. See 'Science by Press Release? An Editorial Response by Barrie Schwortz': http://www.shroud.com/pdfs/schwortzedit01.pdf

Jalsa Salana UK

All of these fascinating views and interpretations of the Shroud have led to the organisations of various Shroud conferences across the world.

I have been fortunate enough to have been directly involved with organising the exhibition at the Jalsa Salana mentioned at the start of this chapter.

At the Jalsa we welcome people of all faiths from all over the world. One feature of the exhibition at Jalsa over the past 5 years has been people with differing views of the Shroud being able to come together and discuss their differences and points of agreement in an open environment.

The mystery of the Shroud remains unsolved. What caused the image to form and what does that tell us about the events surrounding Jesus' Crucifixion? Will another scientific examination of the cloth be permitted where modern technology can be used to analyse the cloth further?

It is questions like these, and the implication of their answers, that has kept people interested in the Shroud of decades and will do so for many decades to come.

Conclusions

At the end of this book, the fruit of passionate research, we can try to offer a rational and synthetic perspective identifying five main scenarios about the possible "Indian years of Jesus".
Indeed in this book we have tried to document:

1) One scenario related with the discovery of Nicholas Notovitch, having its roots in a rich alternative version (that, as it has been reported, spread mostly through oral traditions, in India and less so in the West) of the life of Jesus;
2) An Ahmadiyya Muslim scenario;
3) An esoteric scenario (of unusual visits to the Akashic records),
4) A Hindu scenario (with books as *Natha Namavali Sutra* and *Bhavishya Maha Purana*) and related with founders and scholars of new religious movements born in India (involving important Indian masters as Paramhansa Yogananda, Osho Rajneesh and Satya Sai Baba);
5) Beside supporters of the first scenario, related with Notovitch (and then with the possible stay of Jesus in India during his youth, before the beginning of his Ministry in Palestine) and of the Ahmadiyya Muslim one (and the hypothesis of Jesus life and death, in India, after he had survived the ordeal of crucifixion), there are scholars — Maria Fida Hassnain and Holger Kersten, to offer only two examples — or religious movements — as the *Followers of Jesus* —

claiming that Jesus went to India both before and after the Crucifixion.

Is it reasonable to think they are all legends?

It is a fact — at the moment — that there are no definitive proofs even if, with common sense, we could argue: "where there is smoke there is fire!".

It is also important to mention that there are some significant personalities who support the thesis of Jesus having travelled to India at some point in his life.

I can mention two, among them, of a good calibre.

The first one is Jawaharlal Nerhu, Prime Minister of India after the Independence, in 1947 (to which he has contributed not less than his mystic *alter ego*: Mahatma Gandhi).

Nerhu, has been a well reputed statesman and a good historian. He has authored several books, including the monumental *Glimpses of world history* where he writes:

«It is not clear what Jesus did or where he went before he started his preaching. All over Central Asia, in Kashmir and Ladakh and Tibet and even farther north, there is still a strong belief that Jesus or Isa travelled about there. Some people believe that he visited India also. It is not possible to say anything with certainty, and indeed most authorities who have studied the life of Jesus do not believe that Jesus came to India or Central Asia. But there is nothing inherently improbable in his having done so. In those days the great universities of India, specially Takshashila in the north-west, attracted earnest students from distant countries, and Jesus might well have come there in quest of knowledge. In many respects the teaching of Jesus is so similar to Gautama's teaching that it seems highly probable that he was fully acquainted with it. But Buddhism was sufficiently known in other countries, and Jesus could well have known of it without coming to India»[172].

---

[172]Jawaharlal Nehru, *Glimpses of world history*, Penguin, New Delhi, 2004, p. 98

The other person who I think deserves to be mentioned is Elaine Pagels, Professor of History of Religion at Princeton University, who has great expertise in the field of Gnosticism.

Indeed, she has also authored the book *The Gnostic Gospels* — winning the *National Book Award* and the *National Book Critics Circle Award* — mentioned in the Bibliography.

Elaine Pagels has been interviewed in Paul Davis' movie *Jesus in India* where she affirms: «it is certainly a possibility that the teachings of Jesus are closer or sound closer to what we think are the Indian teachings [...] it's certainly possible, as some people say, that Jesus had travelled to India».

It is also true, as highlights Holger Kersten, that even the "official version" of the life of Jesus presents some important gaps.

Quoting again his book *Jesus lived in India*...

«For fifteen hundred years the only accounts were those which showed Jesus as Saviour along the lines of the official ecclesiastical theology, and which had been written with the specific aim of supportino the faith of contemporary Christians or of converting other people to Christianity.

It was during the Renaissance in Europe that the first critical thinkers emerged, and in the Age of Enlightenment, in the seventeenth and eighteenth centuries, that for the first time studies were published which asked whether Jesus of Nazareth had actually lived.

[...]

Well over 100.000 monographs have since been written on the subject of Jesus, yet the result of all this research into the historical Jesus can only be described as disappointing. Who was Jesus Christ? When wash e born? What did he look like? When was he crucified? When, how and where did he die? The books that were written in the first two centuries of our era contain too few indications to give us any real information about the person Jesus Christ. Later ancient sources are, almost exclusively, ten-

dentious confessions of faith that take for granted a belief in Jesus as the Messiah and Son of God. it is practically impossible to find any really objective testimonies even in the secular literature.
[...]
Christ was certainly born during the reign of Herod, who died four years before our "Christian' era" (that is, in 4 BC!). Jesus' childhood and adolescence are almost entirely ignored in the biblical Gospels although the early years of life are crucial to the forming of a person's character. Even in the nebulous accounts of the short period in which he carried out his public work we find only scanty information about his life. Contemporary historians seem never even to have heard of Jesus»[173].

Tacitus (about AD 55-120), Pliny the Younger (about AD 61-144) and Suetonius (about AD 65-135) mention the Christian sect but they don't give any description of Jesus Christ.

The Jewish Historian Joseph ben Matthias (Ad 37-about 100), who became also a Roman citizen changing his name in Flavius Josephus authored the monumental *The Antiquities of the Jews* in about AD 93, offering crucial details of politics and society at the time of Jesus, mentioning John the Baptist, Herod and Pontius Pilate.

In *The Antiquities of the Jews* "there is only one solitary mention of the name Jesus Christus", referring to the stoning of a man, Jacob, who is mentioned as his brother.

Neither the Jewish writer Justus of Tiberias, a contemporary of Josephus, who extensively wrote about the history of his land has never mentioned Jesus Christ, despite he was living near Capernaum where, according to the Gospels, Jesus often stayed.

---

[173] Holger Kersten, *Jesus lived in India*, op. cit., pp. 19-20.

We find the same silence in the works of Jewish scholar Philo of Alexandria.

Then, writes Kersten, "the one real source for historical research would thus seem to be the collection of scriptures that is the New Testament":

«The New Testament contains four Gospels named after Matthew, Mark, Luke and John. They represent a selection from a much larger number of Gospels that were in use among the various communities and sects of early Christianity before the New Testament was formally put together.
[...]
It remains impossible to determine exactly when and how these Gospels came into being because there is no original text of any of them extant — moreover, there is no clue as to where an orginal might ever have been located. To date them is similarly impossible, even in approximate terms. Th most probable dates, according to the most recent research, are of Mark shortly before AD 70, for Matthew shortly after AD 70, for Luke somewhere between AD 75 and 80 (some authorities would prefer a date closer to AD 100), and it would seem that the Gospel of John was not written until as late as the first decades of the second century. So if Jesus was crucified in around AD 30, the first written records of his existence evidently did not originate until after two or three generations had passed»[174].

Kertsen strongly supports the opinion the biographical value of the Gospels is disputable and that the historical figure of Jesus is sacrificed in favour of his religious image.

At this regard he quotes the Lutheran theologian Rudolf Bultman who affirmed:

---

[174]*Ivi*, pp. 22-23.

«The personality of Jesus, the clear picture of himself and his life, have vanished beyond recall»[175].

Surely with this book I cannot give any definitive contribution to the exciting research to unveil the many mysteries surrounding the life of Jesus.

Mysteries that could potentially involve all the people who are not happy (perhaps only because of a lack of faith) of the dogmatic version.

Then I think this book can simply represent another door opening on another universe and I hope it can inspire other people to start to investigate in the direction of an almost unknown and transcultural Jesus.

Of course, there are many issues to dig deeper in to.

For example, the possible Jewish origin of Afghani and Kashmiri people or the Indian one of the Jews, the authenticity of se-veral documents and facts and much more. Then, further researches should be done on the alleged tomb of Jesus in Srinagar and on the Shroud of Turin.

I really hope our team of researchers can grow and include some academics to join this difficult but fascinating venture.

Then I will end, in a paradoxical manner, with a slogan on French May: *ce n'est qu'un début!*

It is just a beginning and this book is just a starting point. All the signs are there that the journey will continue to be a fascinating one, and the end goal very attractive.

You are all welcome on board; certainly, as it did happen to me in Qadian, we will learn to see the world with a different set of eyes.

---

[175] *Ivi*, pp. 26.

APPENDIX

Shankaracharya Hill or Throne of Solomon?

«The hill has been known in history by many names — Jeetlark, Gopadri, Takht-i-Sulaiman and Shankaracharya Pandit Ratnagar, who precedes the 12th century versifier-historian Kalhana, gives the name of the hill as Jeetlark. He writes that within few days of Raja Narendra ascending the throne a person by the name of Sandiman, who was from "the territories of the Western countries" came to Kashmir and descended on Jeetlark Hill. He writes that Sandiman came flying on his throne and everybody including jins and birds were under his command. Kalhana [author of famous history of Kashmir *Rajtarangini*] mentions the hill by the name of Gopadari and gives an account of the fight between the troops of the then ruler and the pretender Bhiksacara who invaded Srinagar and was repulsed and latter took refuge on the Gopadri hill.
[…]
During the Muslim period the hill was known as Takht-i-Sulaiman (Solomon's Throne) and continued to be called so during the post-Muslim rule in Kashmir commencing with the Sikh reign. The official maps of that period identify the hill as such, as is evidenced by the maps of Kashmir reproduced by Stein from Survey of 1856-60 published in March 1897 by the Survey of India Office, Calcutta [now Kolkata] or another published by Jhon Walker, Geographer to the Secretary of State for India in Council on August 15th 1867. European travelers and officers of the Dogra administration have also mentioned the hill as such in their travelogues and records. William Moorcroft describes it as "the eminence called the Takhti Suliman or the Throne of So-

lomon", The Civil & Military Gazette published as late as in 1935 too describes the hill as Takht-i-Suleiman. This is the name that one profusely comes across in chronicles and travelogues and accounts written by foreign visitors as late as up to the 20th century.

Mughal ruler Jahangir along with his wife, Noor Jahan, once climbed the hill for a picnic on its summit. Noor Jahan is said to have prepared pudding for her husband there upon which Jahangir extempore recited this verse, "Shakar farosh e mann paye halva giri nishast" (My candy seller is seated to prepare the pudding). Noor Jahan equally replied with an extempore verse, "Yani ki zer-i-Takhta-i-Sulaiman pari nishast" (As if a fairy is seated under the [shade of] Solomon's Throne).

Besides the description of Sandiman given by Ratnagar corresponding to the attributes of Prophet Solomon, Bernier [in *Travels in the Mughal Empire*] also refers to an old tradition among the Kashmiris indicating Solomon's arrival in the Valley and having got built a small temple on the hill.

Solomon is credited with delivering the people of Kashmir from inundation of a thousand years when he ordered the accompanying jinns to clear the impediment in the flow of the river [Jhelum]. As they obeyed the command, thus goes the legend, the water flowed out and the Valley emerged.

Since then the shrine on the hill is known as Takht-i-Sulaiman (Solomon's Throne), the hill as Koh-i-Sulaiman (Solomon's Hill) and Kashmir as Bagh-e-Sulaiman (Solomon's Garden).

According to William Wakefield, author of *The Happy Valley: Sketches of Kashmir and The Kashmiris* [London, 1879], Prophet Solomon "is supposed by all good Mussulmans to have taken his stand during the progress of the desiccation of the Valley, carried out by his orders through the means of a spirit or spirits rendered subservient by the Almighty to his will". Abul Fazl mentions the hill as Koh-i-Sulaiman. R.C. Kak believes that "the modern name [Takht-e-Sulaiman] of the hill seems to be of fairly long standing, as it is mentioned by Jesuit Catrou and in a slightly altered form (Koh-i-Sulaiman) by Abul Fazl". Mir Saad Ullah Shahabadi in his versified history of Kashmir titled, *Bagh-e-Sulaiman* (Solomon's Garden) [compiled in 1780] also subscribes to the arrival of Solomon in Kashmir, his landing on the hill and delivering the local people of centuries' inundation. The Persian manuscript of his work is with the Oriental Research Library, Hazratbal. According to Prof. Fida Hassnain [in *Jesus in the East*], the earliest extant records indicate that "Solomon and his architect, Hiram Abiff, had first built the present temple [on the hill] about the same time as completing the Jerusalem Temple". There was a mosque on the summit of the hill adjacent to the stone temple which mysteriously disappeared during the Hindu rule.

The presence of the Muslim worship place alongside the temple has been recorded by the 16th century chronicler, Syed Ali in his *Tareekh-i-Kashmir*.

Francois Bernier, Aurangzeb's physician accompanying the king on his visit to Kashmir in 1665 AD, also mentions "a small Mosque with a garden" atop the hill whose remains were seen by R C Kak, archaeologist and prime minister of the last Dogra ruler, Hari Singh, as late as in 1930s [*The Ancient Monument of Kashmir*].

The mosque being in disuse for long following the advent of the Sikh rule in Kashmir was pulled down possibily in a cleanup operation during Pratap Singh's reign when the renovations of the temple and its electrification works were undertaken. Pratap Singh, through an official order, had also banned entry of Muslims into the temple premises.

Shankaracharya as the name of the hill and the temple atop it is a development which does not go into the past beyond the

mid-19th century. We know that towards the close of the Sikh rule in Kashmir, the shrine was repaired and a new Shivalingam was installed there during the governorship of Sheikh Ghulam Mohiuddin.
According to the officially published *Koshur Encyclopedia*, Vol. 1, the name-change must have taken place at that time. Interestingly, before the Sikh rule in Kashmir there is no historical evidence to suggest that the hill or the temple atop it were known as Shnakaracharya.
In 1961, the Shankaracharya of Dwarika Peeth visited Kashmir and installed the image of Adi Shankaracharya at the temple. Since then, official patronage from calling the hill as Shankaracharya became more pronounced».

In: *greaterkashmir.com*

According to another prestigious source Takht-i-Suleiman «is possibly a 7th century structure which replaced an earlier Buddhist monument of the third century BC traditionally ascribed to Ashoka's son Jhaloka» (In: *www.bl.uk/onlinegallery*)

Biography of Nicholas Notovitch

«Nicolai Alexandrovic Notovitch was born on 25 August 1858 in Kerch, in the Crimea, the second son of a rabbi. Little is known of his childhood, but he evidently received a school education good enough later as a young man to go to the university of St. Petersburg, where his main subject was history. But before that, following the introduction of compulsory military service in Russia in the year 1874, Nicolai Notovitch underwent his military training at the age of about seventeen, and then fought in the Serbian campaign against the Turks in 1876. Soon after this he took part in the Russo-Turkish war (1887-8). It would seem that Notovitch also served in the military during his student days, because in a short notice in the *Daily News* of 23 June 1894 we read that he had been an "officer with the Cossacks".

During the 1880's he wrote and produced a play, *Mariage idéal*, that received some small public acclaim. He was later to write another, called *Gallia*, for which he also composed incidental music.

Notovitch's historical studies had evidently engendered a lively enthusiasm for pan-Slavic ideas. Whereas his brother Osip, who had gained a doctorate as a jurist in St. Petersburg, turned to philosophical and literary pursuits, Nicholai was more interested in the influence of Russian politics on world events. Both brothers nonetheless worked as journalists after their studies. In 1873 Osip Notovitch secured a post as arts editor on a daily newspaper in St. Petersburg.

Later (in 1883), Nicolai was also to work for this daily as correspondent for the Orient. The Notovitch brothers were among those who felt constrained by the acutely anti-Semitic policy of Tsar Alexander III, and this moved Osip to join the Russian Orthodox Church when still a young man. Nicolai must have taken the same step, because he publicly acknowledged his adherence to the Russian Orthodox religion in the French journal *La Paix*.

The year 1887 saw the appearance of Notovitch first publication, a translation in French of a work of a Russian General, which documented his support for the idea of a Franco-Russian alliance.

His second work, published in French in 1890, also dealt with the *Question de l'Alliance Franco-Russe*. In the years 1883 to 1887, as correspondent for the newspaper *Novaya Vremiya*, Notovitch undertook a number of journeys through the Balkans, the Caucaus, Central Asia and Persia.

This lead to a meeting with Aloysius Rotelli (1833-91), who was papal legate in Istanbul from January 1883 until May 1887, and who was later to advise Notovitch as Cardianl in Paris.

In 1887 Notovitch set out his important journey to India, the dates for his stay in Kashmir and Ladakh can be fixed at between 14 October and about 26 November.

His activities thereafter focused mainly on the literary sphere. He stayed for a considerable time in Paris, where from 1889 onwards he published numerous articles in the press — for example in *Le Figaro*, *Le Journal* and *La Science Française*. And it was because Notovitch fully expected publication of the Buddhist story of the life of Jesus to be blocked by the censors in his native land, owing to the restrictive nature of official policy on religious matters there, that he handed his manuscript to a publisher in Paris.

Nevertheless, the first Russian extracts from his book, translated from the German, appeared in 1895 in the journal *Vera i Razum* (N° 22, pp. 575-614), having successfully got past the censor.

Shortly after the appearance of his work *La Vie Inconnue de Jésus Christ*, towards the end of 1895, Notovitch was arrested while on a visit to St. Petersburg, and imprisoned in the Fortress of Peter and Paul.

Accused of literary activity "dangerous to the state and to society", he was exiled without trial to Siberia by the head of a ministry department. His banishment ended in 1897, but even while he was in Siberia Notovitch wrote several articles about his "extraordinary adventure", which appeared anonymously in the journal *La Science Française*. And in his novel *Une Française en Siberie* his main theme was once more the memoirs of a Russian revolutionary.

On his return from an extended journey to Egypt in mid-1898, Notovitch set up a publishing house in Paris to produce the fortnightly journal *La Russie*, which concerned itself primarily with political and economic affairs. In the journal he continued to publish his own essays and reports.

On 2 June 1899, Notovitch was accepted into the celebrated *Société d'Histoire Diplomatique,* the membership of which was made up of high-ranking diplomats and noted historians, and included constituents of the Rotschild family. From 1903 to 1906 Notovitch appears to have stayed in a flat in London, at least intermittently. He then probably returned to Russia. Dating from 1906 there is also an extensive contract drawn up between him and the Shah of Persia detailing the building of roads and pipelines in Iran. In 1910 another Russian edition of the Buddhist story of Jesus' life, *The Life of Saint Issa*, appeared. Up to the year 1916, Notovitch is named in a Russian catalogue of journals as the editor and publisher of various periodicals in St. Petersburg. But after that, not a single trace of Notovitch is to be found anywhere. Perhaps he was keeping a low profile, sheltering from the many attacks mounted by his opponents.

It is even conceivable that the militant agitator was once and for all removed from circulation».

In: Holger Kersten, *Jesus lived in India*, Penguin Books India, New Delhi, 2001, pp. 7-10.

Ahmadiyya Muslim Community; for a violence-free Islam

Ahmadiyya Muslim Community has been founded nearly one hundred and thirty years ago. It has soon spread from its place of origin (India) and, today, it is present worldwide, counting tens of millions of members.
Headquartered in London, it is well reputed in Europe, probably because of its tolerant and nonviolent approach, explicit in its slogan:
Love for all, hatred for none.

Qadian is a small town in Punjab (India) with around forty thousand inhabitants (mostly Muslim and Ahmadiyya). It was founded, in 1530, by Mirzā Hadi Baig, a nobleman of Persian origin. The word *Mirza* (equivalent to *Rajput*) comes from Persian *'Amīrzāde*: son of commander.

The title is a homologue of English *Prince of blood* and of French *Prince du sang,* qualifying a direct descent from imperial families.

Descendant of Mirzā Hadi Baig, Mirzā Ghulām Ahmad (1835-1908) breaks soon the anonymity of his small town.

Short biography of a "new Messiah"

During Mirzā Ghulām Ahmad's childhood, Qadian is considered as a remote village but his father — Mirzā Ghulām Murtaza — is the most prominent landowner, having privileged relationships with political and economic Indian and foreign *élites*. Therefore, Mirzā Ghulām Ahmad has several private tutors, having access to a rich home-library.

Once adult, he doesn't devote much time to professional life or caring about his family business, rather gaining the reputation of a person preferring to live in seclusion.

Indeed, he will spend most of his time studying religious books and praying in the mosques.

He even becomes, day by day, more active in the defense of Islam with exponents of other religions, mostly members of Hindu reform movement Arya Samaj and with Christian missionaries.

In 1889 he asserts he had a divine revelation and to be eligible for an oath of loyalty from the Muslims who would follow him.

With the first oaths sprouts the *Ahmadiyya Muslim Community*, whose founder asserts to be the *Imam Mahdi* (the *divinely* Guided Leader) and the Promised Messiah, awaited in several religious traditions, even among the Muslims.

It should not be left out to briefly mention that the Islamic eschatology foresees the apparition of *Mahdi,* at the end of times, to neutralize the *Dajjāl*: an equivalent of Antichrist.

After the *Mahdi* — or, in Shia traditions, at the same time — will appear Jesus (Isa, in Arabic, whose role, in Islam, is much more important than an average Christian could imagine) who, assembling the forces of virtuous people, will kill the *Dajjāl* and thus becoming the king of the earth for forty years living a perfect Islamic life.

In general, The Holy Quran presents Jesus as a great prophet of God (*rasūlAllāh*) — of human, not divine, nature — born by a virgin and protagonist of several miracles «with Allah's permission».

Jesus, according to the mainstream Islamic tradition, did not die on the cross, rather another man who resembled him was put on the cross, whereas Jesus himself was raised to heaven with his body and soul, living there and coming back to earth in the same person just before judgement day.

He would rule for a few years and then die a natural death (no man, in Islam, is immortal, even Muhammad died in 632), he will be buried in Medina to be resurrected, along with all other humans, on the *Yawm al-dīn* (Day of Judgement) for ultimate divine judgement, when Allah will punish or reward all resurrected dead people, based on their individual deeds and merits.

The worthy people will enjoy the eternal pleasures of *Janna* (paradise) while the damned ones will suffer the temporary *Jahannam* (Islamic hell).

Nevertheless Mirzā Ghulām Ahmad has promoted an heterodox perspective where Jesus, even suffering on the cross, didn't die in that circumstance.

He has been put down when he was just apparently dead or in a coma and he has been brought into the grave by Nicodemus and Joseph of Arimathea.

Treated with an extraordinary powerful ointment (including, among other ingredients, myrrh and aloe) — even mentioned in *The Canon of Medicine* compiled by the Persian philosopher Avicenna and in several other Islamic medical books as Marham-i-Isa (Jesus' ointment) — he soon recovered. Then he met his disciples and he left Palestine in the direction of India with the purpose to meet the lost tribes of Israel (several members of them probably settled in Afghanistan and Kashmir).

Mirzā Ghulām Ahmad has dedicated an entire book (among more than the ninety he wrote) to Jesus' possible journeys after the ordeal of crucifixion whose title could not be more clear: *Jesus in India*.

He has described Jesus' itinerary from Palestine to Kashmir, crossing territories of actual Syria, Persia, Afghanistan and Pakistan. He has even clearly indicated the place where Jesus, in old age (when he was around one hundred and twenty), should have been buried after he died of a natural death: *Rozabal*, (Srinagar's old town).

The claimed natural death of Jesus represents an event of crucial importance in the preaching of Mirzā Ghulām Ahmad.

Indeed, opposed to the mainstream Islamic eschatology that the same (old but living) Jesus would come down from heaven, at the end of times, as a Messiah to the Muslims, Mirzā Ghulām Ahmad asserted that the concerned prophecies should be interpreted in a metaphorical manner.

The new Messiah, in his view, will not be the same person who already came but it would be someone else, with his same nature to affirm similar principles.

Mirzā Ghulām Ahmad, as already anticipated, claimed he has received the revelation to be the chosen one, even in compliance with old prophecies, inaugurating a Messianic age where Islamic principles could affirm through knowledge, persuasion, love for other people (no matter of which religion), strongly refusing any kind of violence.

Rapid growth of Ahmadiyya Community

Mirzā Ghulām Ahmad announced to be the promised Messiah and *Mahdi* in 1891. At the end of that year — on December twenty-seventh, twenty-eighth and twenty-ninth — in Qadian there was the first *Jalsa Salana (annual gathering)*: the annual meeting of *Ahmadiyya Muslim Community*.

It involved just seventy-five people.

Nevertheless, the number of participants to the *Jalsa Salana* grew till two thousand in 1907.

In 1908, a day after Mirzā Ghulām Ahmad's death, the community elected Hakeem Noor-ud-Din as his *khalifah* ("successor").

In 1914, when the first *khalifah* passed away, Ahmad's son, Mirza Basheer-ud-Din Mahmood Ahmad was elected.

The young successor was not accepted by all members, causing one split and the creation of the minority *Ahmadiyya Movement of Lahore*, defined by sociologist Massimo Introvigne: «nearer to traditional Islam.

His members try to spread its message in the West with some adaptation and less emphasis on the messianic nature of the founder who is, anyway, venerated».

In 1946, one year before India's independence and the consequent partition giving origin to Western and Eastern Pakistan, the participants to the annual *Jalsa Salana* of *Ahmadiyya Muslim Community* were around forty thousand.

In 1948 the Community transfers its headquarters to Rabwah, in Pakistan and, then, annual meetings started to be organized there, with an increasing number of participants.

The life of *Ahmadiyya Muslim Community* becomes more difficult since 1974 when, in Pakistan, the parliament, by the help of seventy-two Islamic sects declare, unanimously, that Ahmadies cannot be considered as Muslims.

One decade after, crucial changes in the Pakistani Penal Code forbid Ahmadiesnot only to spread their "heterodox" perspectives but forbade them even to remotely "pose" as Muslims.

Section 298-C of 1984 Ordinance XX, for example, contemplates a punishment for up to three years imprisonment for«Any person of the Quadiani group or the Lahori group (who call themselves 'Ahmadis' or by any other name), who, directly or indirectly, poses himself as Muslim, or calls, or refers to, his faith as Islam, or preaches or propagates his faith, or invites others to accept his faith, by words, either spoken or written, or by visible representations, or in any manner whatsoever outrages the religious feelings of Muslims».

Because of following persecutions and arrests, in 1984, the then head of the community, the fourth *khalīfah*, moves to London and many Ahmadis are forced to ask for political asylum in Western countries (among those especially in Germany, where Ahmadiyya now are the first Muslim Community to be officially recognized as a public entity).

The Ahmadis are considered as heretic by other Muslims because, in addition to a different eschatological perspective, their founder has been accused to have reopened the prophetic cycle, which, according to Sunni and Shiite traditions, has ended with the figure of Muhammad.

Although Mirzā Ghulām Ahmad, speaking of himself as prophet, clearly indicates that his prophethood is merited by fully following the prophet Muhammad and is not a new or law-giving prophethood, but a limited one, referring to direct communication with Allah.

Nowadays the Ahmadis have to face severe opposition not just in Pakistan. The Wahabi government of Saudi Arabia doesn't allow them to do the pilgrimage to Mecca and they are victims of persecutions also in Bangladesh, Indonesia, Kirghizistan and, most recently, in Algeria.

Today the Community is led by the fifth *khalīfah*, Hazrat Mirza Masroor Ahmad, elected in 2003.

He lives in London and his Friday sermons are broadcast from the Baitul Futuh Mosque live to the whole community through their own satellite channel MTA International.

The *Ahmadiyya Muslim Community*, according to its official website *alislam.org*, has promoted the construction of around fifteen thousand mosques, five hundred schools and more than thirty hospitals worldwide.

Its members have translated The Holy Quran in more than seventy languages and they spread the teachings of Islam and messages of peace and tolerance through their TV channel MTA, their website and the publishing house *Islam International Publications*.

They are also very active in the humanitarian field with NGO *Humanity First*.

With a growing Muslim presence in the West, it is probable that the message and the activities of *Ahmadiyya Muslim Community* will arouse, day by day, more interest.

Record of the Going of I'sa — U.W.B., etc. — to the region of Nassibin and the resuscitation of Sam the son of Nuh — U.W.B., etc. — by the prayers of his Lordship, U.W.B., etc.

Historians have reported that in the time of I'sa — U.W.B., etc. — there was a king in the country of Nassibin who was very arrogant and tyrannical. I'sa having been sent on a mission to him, started towards Nassibin. When he arrived in the vicinity, he halted and said to his apostles: "Which of you will enter the city and say: I'sa, who is a servant of Allah, His messenger and His word, is coming to you". One of them, whose name was Ya qub, exclaimed: "I will go, O spirit of Allah". The Lord I'sa said: "Go, although thou art the first who wilt separate thyself from me". After that another monotheist, Tuman by name, asked permission to accompany Ya qub. I'sa allowed him to do so, but said: "O Tuman, thou art predestined soon to be afflicted". The Shima'un said: "O spirit of Allah, if thou wilt permit, I shall be the third of them, on condition that in case of trouble, when I invoke thy aid, thou wilt not withhold it". After he had also obtained leave the three men departed. Shima'un tarried outside the city, saying to his companions: "Enter ye, and do that which I'sa hath ordered you. If any misfortune befall you, I shall try to remedy it". Before they arrived in Nassibin the foes of religion had spread evil reports about I'sa and his mother, so that when Tuman and Ya qub entered the city, and the latter individual raised the shout, "Verily now I'sa, the spirit of Allah, and His word, His servant and His first messenger [or apostle], has come to you", the people turned towards him and asked: "Who of you two is the speaker of these words?" Ya qub disavowed these words, and denied having uttered them, but Tuman [on the contrary] said: "I have spoken these words". The people then accused him of falsehood, and uttered unbecoming sentiments with reference to I'sa and to Mariam. They led Tuman to the king, who ordered him to revoke these words on pain of death.

Tuman refused to comply, whereon the tyrant commanded his hands and feet to be cut off, his eyes to be pierced with an awl, and his body to be thrown upon a dunghill. When Shima'un had heard what took place, he entered the city, waited upon the king and said: "I hope the benignity of your majesty will grant me the permission to ask a few questions from a man who has been punished". The king having assented, Shima'un went to the dunghill and asked Tuman: "What are thy words?". He replied: "I say that I'sa is the spirit of Allah, His servant and His messenger". Shima'un continued: "What are thy arguments in favour of the truth of these words?" Tuman replied: "He heals those who are blind from birth, lepers and all kind of diseases". Shima'un continued: "Physicians do these things likewise, and are participators in such acts. What other sign does he possess?".

Tuman said: "He knows what people eat in their houses and what they put aside".

Shima'un rejoined: "Soothsayers do this. Is there any other sign in him?". Tuman said: "He makes a bird of clay, breathes into it, and it begins to fly". Shima'un said: "This looks like sorcery. What other arguments has he in favour of his pretension?". He replied: "By the permission of Allah — w.n.b.e. — he can resuscitate a dead man to life again".

Shima'un then made the following report to the king, saying: "This culprit speaks of great things performed by I'sa, and which can originate only form the Omnipotent and Absolute Sovereign, or from His prophet. Any act of a messenger [i.e., apostle] also depends upon the permission of the Lord of lords, nor would the Eternally-living One allow any sorcerer to work such miracles. If I'sa be not a messenger of Allah, he cannot revive a dead body; therefore the best will be to call I'sa and to try him whether he can do all that this man asserts; but if I'sa refuses to comply, thou mayest [safely] chastise the man whom he has sent with any [additional] punishment thou mayest deem fit. If, on the other hand, I'sa resuscitates a dead man, we shall be obliged to believe in him, because the resuscitation of the dead will be a convincing argument and an invincible proof of his being a true prophet and a messenger [of God]". The king approved of what Shima'un had said and ordered the spirit of Allah [i.e. Jesus] to be produced. I'sa — U.W.B., etc. — came and by his advent the assembly received new luster and freshness. The king the ordered Shima'un to converse and so dispute with I'sa, to whom Shima'un accordingly said in the presence of the king: "This thy envoy, who has incurred the wrath of our king, bears testimony that thou art a messenger of Allah". I'sa replied: "He speaks the truth". Shima'un continued: "He imagines thou art able to heal those who are blind from birth and lepers, as well as that thou curest sick persons". I'sa replied: "His assertion is in conformity with facts". Shima'un rejoined: "It has been decided that if thou canst not perform that which Tuman pretended concerning thee, we shall kill thee and thy companions". I'sa said: "Yes". Shima'un asked: "Then begin with thy companion". I'sa thereon placed the hands and feet of Tuman, which had been amputated, upon their stumps and drew his own hands over them, whereon, by the power of Allah, Tuman became whole as before. Then he rubbed his blessed hands upon the eyes of Tuman and he began to see. Shima'un exclaimed: "O king, this is a sign of the signs of his being a prophet". Then Shima'un begged I'sa — U.W.B., etc. — to reveal what those present in the assembly had been eating last night, and what they had put aside. The Messiah — U.W.B., etc. — then accosted each man separately and told him what he had eaten the past evening and what he had laid aside. Shima'un again said: "Thy envoy imagines that thou makest of clay the similitude of a bird and after breathing into it, thou causest it to fly; and the king whishes to behold this strange event". I'sa asked: "The figure of what bird is wanted?". They said, "The bat, because it is a strange bird". Accordingly he fashioned it, breathed on it and it flew.

It is related after Solman, the Persian, that when all the sick of Nassibin had been healed, the people requested I'sa to resuscitate a dead man. His lordship said: :Whatever deceased person you may point out, I shall recall him to life by the permission of the Living Immortal One". They said: "Sam, the son of Nuh, is our ancestor; his corpse is not far from this place, if thou conentest to resuscitate it by thy sublime breathings". I'sa agreed and the people conducted him to a tomb, where the spirit of Allah [i.e. Jesus] fell on his knees, raising his hands in supplication. After he had terminated his devotions, he called out to Sam, by the command of the Creator of heaven and earth, whereon the soil moved and opened, when a man with a grey head and beard issued from the tomb, and said: "I obey, O spirit of Allah". Then he harangued those present as follows: "O people, this is I'sa, the son of the blessed virgin Mariam, the spirit of Allah, and His word which he is preaching. You must believe in his prophetic dignity, and follow him". I'sa asked Sam: "In your time the hair of men never became gray; how is this [that yours is so]?". He replied: "When I heard thy voice, I thought that the resurrection was at hand and I was so awed that my hair turned gray". I'sa again asked: "How many years is it since thou art dead?". Sam replied: "Four thousand years". I'sa continued: "I shall pray that Allah — u.w.b.e — may allow thee to live some time". Sam [however] replied:

"Since it will, after all, be necessary to taste the unpleasant beverage of death, I wish not for this miserable life, and I still remember my agonies of death. I beseech thee to implore the Almighty — w.n.b.e.— to receive me into the propinquity of His mercy". I'sa then prayed, Sam returned to his former condition, and the particles of earth again united [and covered him]. Solman the Persian narrated that when the King of Nassibin and his people had witnessed this miracle, he with his army, followers and subjects believed in I'sa[177].

---

[177] In: *Rauzat Us Safa*, Vol. II, London, 1982, pp. 165-169.

Bibliography

Ahmad Al Haj Khwaja Nazir, *Jesus in heaven on earth*, Muslim Mission and Literary Trust, 1956.
Ahmad Mirza Ghulām, *Jesus in India*, Rabwa, Pakistan, The Ahmadiyya Muslim Foreign Missions Department, 1899.
Al-Said-us-Sadiq Abi Jaffar Muhammad [...] Al Shaikh, *Ikmal-ud-Din*, Iran, Syed-us-Sanad Press, 1782.
Anand Krishna, *Christ of kashmiris*, Anand Ashram Foundation (in collaboration with Anand Krishna Global Cooperation), Indonesia, 2008.
Baigent Michael, *The Jesus papers*, Harper, San Francisco, 2006.
Batchelor Stephen, *The awakening of the West. The encounter of Buddhism and Western culture*, HarperCollins, London, 1994.
Bengalee Sufi Mutiur Rahman, *The tomb of Jesus*, The Moslem Sunrise Press, 1946.
Bennett Clinton, *In search of Jesus*, Continuum, London & New York, 2001.
Berna Kurt, *Christ did not perish on the cross*, Zurich, International Foundation for the Holy Shroud, 1975.
Beskov Per, *Strange tales about Jesus*, Fortress Press, Philadelphia, 1985.
Bipin Chandra Pal, *Memories of my life and times,* Bipin Chandra Pal Institute, Calcutta, 1973.
Bipin Chandra Pal, *The soul of India,* The New Indian Printing & Publishing Co LTD, Calcutta, 1940.
Black Matthew, *The scrolls and Christian origins*, London, Thomas Nelson & Sons LTD, 1961.
Bock Janet, *The Jesus Mystery*, Sawbridge, 1985.

Borg Marcus J., *Jesus: a new vision*, San Francisco, Harper and Row Publishers, 1987.
Brunton Paul, *A search in secret India*, Arrow, London, 1965.
Burke O.M., *Among the dervishes*, The Octagon Press, London, 1993.
Chaudhary Aziz A., *Jesus among the lost sheeps*, Islam International Publications LTD.
Chowdhuri Dhirendranath, *In search of Jesus Christ*, B.M. Press, Calcutta, 1927.
Clare Prophet Elizabeth, *The lost years of Jesus*, Book Faith, New Delhi, 1994.
Coomaraswamy Ananda K., *Buddha and the Gospel of Buddhism*, G.P. Putnam's Sons, New York, 1916.
Craig William Lane, *The Historical Argument for the Resurrection of Jesus during the Deist controversy*, Lewiston, NY: Edwin Mellen Press, 1985.
Dasgupta Ansupati and Kunja Bihari Kundu, *Swami Abhedananda's Journey into Kashmir and Tibet*, Ramakrishna Vedanta Math, Calcutta, 1987.
Davies, Dr. Trevor & Margaret, "Resurrection or Resuscitation", *Journal of the Royal College of Physicians of London*, April, 1991.
Deardorff James, *Jesus in India*, Lanham: International Scholars Publications, 1995.
Derret, J. Duncan M, *The Anastasis: The Resurrection of Jesus as an Historical Event*, Shipston-on-Stour, Warwickshire, England: P. Drinkwater, 1982.
Doniger Wendy, *The Hindus, an alternative history*, Speaking Tiger Publishing, New Delhi, 2015.
Dupuche John, R., *The Abhinavagupta Kula Ritual, as elaborated in Chapter 29 of the Tantraloka*, Motilal Banarsidass, New Delhi, 2003.
Eliade Mircea, *Cosmos and history, the myth of eternal return*, Harper & Brothers, New York, 1959.

Eliade Mircea, *The Encyclopedia of Religion*, Macmillan Publishing Company, New York, 1987.
Eliade Mircea and Ioan P. Coulianu, *The Harper Collins concise guide to world religions*, Harper San Francisco, San Francisco, 1991.
Elliott J.K., *The Apocryphal New Testament*, Clarendon Press, Oxford, 1993.
Faber-Kaiser Andreas, *Gesù visse e morì in Cascemir*, De Vecchi Editore, Milano, 1978.
Feuerstein G. et al., *In search of the cradle of civilization*, Quest Books, Wheaton, Ill., USA, Adyar, Madras, India, 1995.
Finegan Jack, *Hidden records of the life of Jesus*, Philadelphia, Pilgrim Press, 1969.
Fugairon L.S.-Bricaud J., *La Santa Gnosi; Esposizione delle dottrine e dei riti della Chiesa Gnostica Universale*, Atanor, Todi, 1922.
Furst Jeffrey, *Edgar Cayce's story of Jesus*, Neville, Spearman, London, 1968.
Gibbons Bob-Sian Pritchard Jones, *Ladakh land of magical monasteries,* Pilgrims Publishing, Varanasi, 2006.
Goddard Dwight, *Was Jesus influenced by Buddhism?*, White River Junction, Vermont, Charles H. Cummings, 1927.
Goel Sita Ram, *Jesus Christ, an artifice for aggression*, Voice of India, New Delhi, 1994.
Hassnain Maria Fida-Dahan Levi, *The Fifth Gospel*, Destgir Publications, Srinagar (Kashmir-India), 1988.
Hassnain Maria Fida-Dahan Levi, *Jesus in the East, incredible saga*, Destgir Publications, Srinagar (Kashmir-India), 2002.
Hassnain Maria Fida, *A search for historical Jesus*, Destgir Publications, Srinagar (Kashmir-India), 2003.
Ishavardas Fakeer, *Jesus the true master yogi*, Grace Books, Bathinda, Punjab, India.

Jacobs Alan, *When Jesus lived in India*, Watkins Publishing, London, 2009.
Josephus Flavius, *The Works of Flavius Josephus*, translated by William Whiston, Wesley.nnu.edu/josephus.
Kalhana, *Rajtarangini*, Sahitya Akademi, New Delhi, 1990.
Kashmiri Aziz, *Christ in Kashmir*, Srinagar, Roshni Publications, 1984.
Kersten Holger & Gruber Elmar, *The original Jesus*, Element Books LTD, Shaftesbury, Dorset, 1995.
Kersten Holger & Gruber Elmar, *The Jesus conspiracy*, Barnes & Noble Books, New York, 1995.
Kersten Holger, *Jesus lived in India*, Penguin, New Delhi, 2001.
Khan Muhammad Zafrulla, *Deliverance from the cross*, London, The London Mosque, 1978.
Khawand Shah Ibn-i-Muhammad, Mir Muhammad, *Rauzatus-Safa fi Sirat-ul-Ambia wal Muluk wal Khulafa* ("Garden of Purity concerning the biography of the Prophets and Kings and Caliphs"), Bombay, 1852 (originally written in 1417).
Laszlo Erwin, *Science and the Akashic Field*, Inner Traditions, Rochester, Vermont (USA), 2007.
Levi H. Dowling, *The Aquarian Gospel of Jesus Christ*, L.N. Fowler & CO. LTD, London, 1972.
Levi H. Dowling, *The Aquarian Gospel of Jesus Christ; the missing years*, Watkins Publishing, London, 2010.
Lillie Arthur, *Buddhism in Christendom*, London, 1887.
Lillie Arthur, *India in primitive Christianity*, London, 1909.
Malleson G.B., *History of Afghanistan*, London, 1878.
Masood Steven, *Jesus and the Indian Messiah*, World of life, Oldham (UK), 1994.
Medlycott A.D., *India and the apostle Thomas. An inquiry with a critical analysis of the Acta Thomae*, London, Davide Nutt, 1905.
Meer Izzut-Oollah, *Travels in central Asia*, Calcutta, 1872.

Menon A. Sreedhara, *A survey of Kerala history*, Sahitya Pravarthaka Co-operative Society LTD, Kottayam (Kerala State, India), 1967.
Meurois-Givaudan Anne & Daniel, *The Hidden Face of Jesus from Essene Memory*, Amrita Editions, 1991.
Nehru Jawaharlal, *Glimpses of world history*, Penguin, New Delhi, 2004.
Notovitch Nicholas, *The Unknown Life of Jesus Christ*, Hachette India, Gurgaun, 2013.
Olivares Manuel, *Gesù in India?*, Viverealtrimenti, 2015
Pagels Elaine, *The Gnostic Gospels*, Pelican Books, London, 1982.
Pappas Paul C., *Jesus tomb in India, the debate on his death and resurrection*, Asian Humanities Press, Berkley, California, 1991.
Paramahansa Yogananda, *The second coming of Christ* (Vol. I, II), Yogoda Satsanga Society of India, 2007.
Paramahansa Yogananda, *The Yoga of Jesus*, Self Realization Fellowship, Los Angeles, 2007
Potter Charles Francis, *The lost years of Jesus revealed*, Greenwich, Connecticut, Fawcet Publications, INC, 1962.
Prinsep Henry T., *Tibet, Tartary and Mongolia*, London, 1852.
Rae George Milne, *The Syrian church in India*, London, William Blackwood and sons, 1892.
Rajneesh Osho, *The Rajneesh Bible*, Rajneesh Foundation International, Rajneeshpuram, Oregon (USA)Vol I, 1985.
Read Anne, *Edgar Cayce on Jesus and his church*, Warner Books, New York, 1970.
Renan Ernest, *Life of Jesus*, Watts & Co, London, 1904.
Rev. C.C. Dobson, *Did our Lord Visit Britain as they say in Cornwall and Somerset?*, The Avalon Press, Glastonbury, 1947.
Roerich Nicholas, *Altai-Himalaya*, Book Faith India, Delhi, 1996.

Roerich Nicholas, *Heart of Asia*, Pilgrims Publishing, Varanasi, 2007.
Salahuddin Abunakr Ben Ishmael, *Saving the savior. Did Christ survive the crucifixion?*, Jammu Press, Evanston (Illinois – U.S.), 2001.
Sanghi Ashwin, *The Rozabal line*, Westland LTD, New Delhi, 2008.
Sastry K.S. Ramaswamy, *The Tamils and their culture*, Annamalai University, Annamalainagar, 1967.
Schonfield Hugh, *The Passover plot*, Bantam Books, London New York/Toronto, 1969.
Schonfield Hugh, *The Essene odyssey*, Element Books, Longmead, UK, 1984.
Schweitzer Albert, *The quest of historical Jesus*, SCM, London, 1954.
Serrano Miguel, *The serpent of paradise, the story of an Indian pilgrimage*, RKP, London, 1974.
Shams J.D., *Where did Jesus die?*, Lahore, Ripon Printing Press, 1960.
Sykes P., *A history of Afghanistan*, Vol. I-II, Macmillan & Co, London, 1940.
Singh Nag Sharan, *Bhavisya Mahapuranam*, Jawahar Nagar, Delhi: Nag Publisher, 1984 (originally compiled in 115 A.D.).
Singhal D.P., *India and World civilization*, Michigan State University Press, 1969 (Rupa, New Delhi, 2014).
Smith W., *A comprehensive dictionary of the Bible*, D. Appleton and Company, New York, 1871.
Smith W. et al., *A dictionary of Christian antiquities*, John Murray, London, 1875.
Spencer H. Lewis, *The mystical life of Jesus*, San Jose, California (Rosicrucian Library), Supreme Grand Lodge of AMORC, 1982.

Spong John Shelby, *Resurrection: Myth or Reality*, Harper, San Francisco, 1994.
Spong John Shelby, *Why Christianity may change or die*, Harper, San Francisco, 1998.
Steiner Rudolf, *The Fifth Gospel, Investigation of the Akasha Chronicle*, Rudolpf Steiner Publishing Co., London, 1950
Stroud William, *On the physical cause of the death of Christ*, London: Hamilton, Adams & Co.; Glasgow: T.D., Morrison, 1871.
Swami Abhedananda, *Complete works*, Ramakrishna Vedanta Math, Calcutta, 1967.
Swami Abhedananda, *Journey into Kashmir and Tibet*, Ramakrishna Vedanta Math, Calcutta, 2001.
Swami Paramananda, *Christ and Oriental ideals*, Boston, Vedanta Centre, 1923.
Swami Rama Tirtha, *In woods of God-realization*, Vol. I-IV, Rama Tirtha Pratisthan, Lucknow, 1956.
Swami Rama Tirtha, *In woods of God realisation*, Imperial Book Depot Press, Delhi, 1911.
Swami Sivananda, *Lives of saints*, The Sivananda Publication League, Rishikesh, 1947.
Swami Sivananda, *Life and teachings of Lord Jesus*, The Divine Life Society, Shivanandanagar (Dist. Tehri-Garhwal, Uttaranchal, India), 2006.
Thomas M.M., *The acknowledged Christ of Indian renaissance*, Madras, 1976.
Thundy Zacharias P., *Buddha and Christ: Nativity stories and Indian traditions*, New York: E.J. Brill, 1993.
Tsering N., *The monasteries of Hemis, Chemde and Dagthag*, New Delhi.
Tucci Giuseppe, *The religions of Tibet*, Routledge and Kegan, London, 1980.
Wilson Ian, *The blood and the shroud*, New York, The free press, 1998.

Yasin Mohammad, *Rauzabal and other mysteries of Kashmir*, Srinagar, Kesar Publisher, 1972.
Zafrulla Khan Muhammad, *Deliverance from the cross*, The London Mosque, 1978.

Al Qur'an, The Institute of Islamic Knowledge, USA, 1997.
An eastern view of Jesus Christ, Divine Discourses of Sathya Sai Baba, Sai Publications, London, 1982.
Le origini dello gnosticismo; colloquio di Messina 13-18 Aprile 1966, E.J.Brill, Leiden, 1967.
New Testament Apocrypha, James Clarke & Co, Cambridge, 1992.
Parliament of religions, Swami Vivekananda centenary, Calcutta, 1966.
The Crucifixion, By An Eye-Witness, Indo-American Book Co, Chicago, 1915.
The periplus of the Erythraean sea, The Hakluyt Society, London, 1980.
The Septuagint Bible, The Falcon's wing press, Indian Hills, Colorado, 1954.